Roadmap to Strategic HR

Roadmap to Strategic HR

Turning a Great Idea into a
Business Reality

Ralph Christensen

Foreword by Dave Ulrich

⁴AMACOM

American Management Association

New York • Atlanta • Brussels • Chicago • Mexico City • San Francisco
Shanghai • Tokyo • Toronto • Washington, D.C.

Special discounts on bulk quantities of AMACOM books are available to corporations, professional associations, and other organizations. For details, contact Special Sales Department, AMACOM, a division of American Management Association, 1601 Broadway, New York, NY 10019.
Tel.: 212-903-8316. Fax: 212-903-8083.
Web site: www.amacombooks.org

This publication is designed to provide accurate and authoritative information in regard to the subject matter covered. It is sold with the understanding that the publisher is not engaged in rendering legal, accounting, or other professional service. If legal advice or other expert assistance is required, the services of a competent professional person should be sought.

Library of Congress Cataloging-in-Publication Data

Christensen, Ralph
    Roadmap to strategic HR : turning a great idea into a business reality / Ralph Christensen.
        p.   cm.
    Includes bibliographical references and index.
    ISBN-10: 0-8144-0867-2
    ISBN-13: 978-0-8144-0867-4
    1. Personnel management.   2. Personnel departments—Management.
3. Manpower planning.   4. Strategic planning.   5. Personnel management—
Vocational guidance.   I. Title: Roadmap to strategic human resources.
II. Title.

HF5549.C457   2006
658.3'01—dc22

                                                                2005009556

Printing Hole Number

10   9   8   7   6   5   4   3

Contents

Foreword
Roadmap to Strategic HR:
Turning a Great Idea into a Business Reality

ANYONE WHO HAS BEEN on a long trip with children has heard the question, "Are we there yet?" In many ways, HR professionals have been asking this question for the past 30 years: "Are we there yet?" Are we (HR professionals) able to help turn strategy into action? Are we able to quantify the value we create, and to justify our continued existence? Are we valued in the eyes of the line managers we serve? Are we able to move beyond our legacy and history of administration, and become truly strategic?

To define "there," we need both a destination where we are headed and a roadmap for getting from here to there. As the field of HR bifurcates into two parts (transaction and transformation), defining "there" becomes a bit more complex and more important than ever. The transaction work of HR defines what has been, and often still is, the description of "there" for HR. Managing payroll, administering benefits, coordinating company events, negotiating employee contracts, handling staffing logistics, ensuring legal compliance, and monitoring training classes have historically been the focus of HR work.

Now many of these standardized and routine activities are being done by HR policy specialists in service centers, by employees themselves through Web-based technology, or by external vendors through outsourcing contracts. As the transaction work gets done better, faster, and cheaper, HR professionals now must shift their attention and focus. "There" has shifted from doing transaction and administrative work more efficiently to delivering strategic and transformation work more effectively.

The HR transition from transaction to transformation requires new thinking, models, practices, and competencies. Many continue to judge HR's relevance for today's business by yesterday's activities. And HR falls short. Today's business demands that organizations have capabilities of agility, speed, innovation, collaboration, talent, and resilience. Against these standards, traditional HR with a focus on administrative routines fails to deliver. And too often HR is stereotyped as only doing this transaction work. Like actors who have become typecast, many HR professionals cannot break out of their traditional roles. In this light, the legacy of HR with a focus on administrative tasks keeps HR from delivering strategic value. HR professionals are seen as less relevant (delivering administrative work that can be done better in other ways) and not seen as competent or committed to the strategic side of the business.

And the need for transformational HR is greater than ever. In a global economy, with customers having ever-increasing choices, with technology changing the rules of both the design and delivery of products and services, with changing demographics in the workforce, and with information ubiquity, business leaders have learned that they must adapt to new rules of competition. Competitiveness is no longer a formal strategy with a product focus and three-year capital plans. Competitiveness requires that leaders create organizational capabilities to match strategic intents, engage people fully in the business, and move ideas quickly across boundaries. These new organizational capabilities become the deliverables for HR. They shape the agenda for HR professionals who want to turn in their traditional administrative roles for ones centered on creating strategic value.

But this new "there" in HR is easier to define in theory than enact in practice. It is easier to conceptualize, conceive, and write about utopia than to actually make it happen. Many of the images of the new

HR enthuse in principle, but are terribly difficult to accomplish in practice.

Ralph Christensen's book *Roadmap to Strategic HR: Turning a Great Idea into a Business Reality* is a major step toward defining "there" for the new HR. I have known Ralph for almost 30 years. Sometimes formally trained academics have conceptual insight without practical relevance. Ralph is the opposite. Thirty years ago, when some of us chose to go into academics and live more in the world of ideas, Ralph chose to go into the world of practice. To be honest, he was then and is now one of the best "thinkers" in the profession. He has not required a Ph.D. to hone his observation skills and analytic ability. He has always been gifted at simultaneously doing the day-to-day work that HR leaders must do while conceiving the more abstract principles required to direct and do it well. He is more of an academic in the purest form than many of my colleagues because he returns again and again to fundamental principles on which action is based. And he has shown repeatedly that he can turn ideas into action in aerospace, digital, consulting, and consumer products fields. This unique combination of skills allows his book to be not just another case study of HR innovation, but a story that draws and builds on principles that define the future of HR. In his book, he synthesizes much of the conceptual work on HR, then reports how these principles can be put into practice.

This book offers a reader's digest of some of the latest thinking in HR. It will also help those interested in turning HR ideas into action in a number of ways:

- Understanding why HR should focus on transformational work. Building the case for the new HR starts by understanding new business realities like globalization, customer choice, technological change, and employee diversity. Ralph helps the HR professional through this data, and then frames conversations with business leaders to show that HR expertise will help business leaders reach their goals.

- Defining the "strategic" HR role with specific actions. With personal examples from Digital, Martin Marietta, Watson Wyatt, and Hallmark, Ralph points out that strategic HR is not a long-term venture always waiting to happen, but a series of today's choices around people and people practices. He wisely weaves traditional organizational development (OD) and change programs into the new HR, and shows how transformation requires competence in not only people practices like staffing and compensation, but in OD work like large-scale system change.

- Offering ten specific steps for getting from here (today's HR work) to there (strategic HR work). Each step is rooted in practice with examples and experiences that have worked (and in some cases, not worked). Each step has questions, tools, and frameworks that help the reader not only understand the idea, but the action it requires. These steps are a useful template for an HR leader seeking to actually do strategic HR work.

Many of the specific tools will help an HR leader know the current status of the organization and how to move forward:

- HR readiness assessment (Chapter 3) helps define the likelihood of success, and where to focus attention to be ready for HR transformation.

- HR's five fundamental processes (Chapter 4) lays out where HR can have impact, and offers specific HR practices that can be framed in a strategic way (Chapters 8–13).

- Characteristics of an effective vice president of human resources (Chapter 5) suggests competencies required for HR professionals.

- Elements of an HR plan (Chapter 7) provides a template for how to focus HR attention.

- Laying out the roles for HR professionals (Chapter 14) (architect, change agent, HR generalist, HR specialist).

- Showing how to design the structure and reporting relationship of the new HR organization (Chapter 15).

- Suggesting competencies for the HR professional (Chapter 16).

- Navigating the process for implementing the new HR (Chapter 17), and suggesting what HR careers will look like (Chapter 18).

For each of these topics, Ralph shares his experiences and insights into how he wrestled with these issues and helped turn ideas into action. These elegant case studies will likely help others who experience similar challenges.

So, are we there yet? I don't think so, not yet. However, Wayne Brockbank, one of my close colleagues, quietly said to me the other day, "What happens when firms actually do the strategic HR work we have been talking about for years? Will we will have a job?" My first instinct was to belittle the question and assert, "No one will ever get there. We will always have impact." But upon further reflection, with books like Ralph's, the "there" is getting clearer all the time, and the path to get there is also becoming clearer. As more firms adapt the conceptual ideas about strategic HR, and find ways to implement them, the gap shrinks between the HR aspiration to be strategic and its ability to be so. Think of the March of Dimes, which built an organization of ridding the world of polio. That organization had to reinvent itself when polio was essentially cured. Over time, HR's leading thinkers will slowly realize that many business leaders already practice good-people-management skills, and that strategic HR must address other business challenges to help create more competitive organizations. At this point in our professional development, getting more clarity about strategic HR is a worthy and worthwhile venture, and this book helps us actually make it happen.

Dave Ulrich
Montreal
April 2005

Preface

NOT LONG AGO, I met with a CEO who couldn't imagine why he would invite his head of HR to become a regular part of the business team. Although this CEO saw the value of people issues to his business, he simply didn't believe that HR could add value to the business team as they grappled with significant issues. He, like too many other CEOs, was hopelessly biased by a belief that the HR group provides only administrative support. Since this is the only exposure to HR that some CEOs have known, too many don't expect, and therefore don't, facilitate a stronger, more vital HR group.

In contrast, I recently heard the CEO and the senior HR leader of a fast-growing retail business speak together about the company's strategy. It was thrilling. The CEO spoke eloquently about the human resources strategy and why he was so dependent upon HR fulfilling a critical role in the company's aggressive strategy. The VP-HR was just as passionate and articulate as the CEO about the marketplace, the competition, financial models, and what their company needed to do to win. It was clear that they were a team. Though that quality of business partnership is more often seen today than it was ten years ago, it doesn't occur often enough.

Many in HR believe that HR should play a strategic role in the business, and they have picked up the vocabulary that reflects those ideas. But there still are too few HR leaders who are ready to step in and play that role. Why do these gaps exist? It certainly isn't because the need isn't real. It isn't due to a lack of intelligent, hardworking people in these HR roles.

In my experience, the primary reason that there is still such a large gap between the theory and practice of strategic human resources is that too few HR professionals have a clear picture in their minds of what these ideas look like in application. They like the theory. They believe that the people equation of a business can make a huge difference. They would love to step up and play a more influential role. Some even convince themselves that they are playing that type of influential role. But too many can't translate the theory into action. Too many have been tutored only by those who see the function as primarily administrative. They just can't quite see it. Until they can envision the theory being applied, they are not likely to play a stronger contributing role.

This book begins to fill the gap between strategic human resources theory and practice. Many in the field have skillfully made the case for *why* we need a more strategic HR function in organizations. Others have worked for decades on *what* makes up the "technologies" of various human resources domains. The space in between deals with *how* does one actually make it work.

I am offering HR professionals and line leaders a practical way to think about implementing great human resources theory. I provide specific frameworks that must be in place to transform human resources work and roles in an organization. And I give concrete examples of how to design, manage, and implement these frameworks.

I have written this book as though I were having a stimulating informal conversation with a group of colleagues exploring one another's learnings and experiences in making strategic human resources a reality. Such a conversation would undoubtedly deal with a variety of models, but would focus quickly on experiences—both those that worked and those that did not. I often wish that there were more such forums available for HR colleagues.

I do not include a great deal of research. There are others who do that remarkably well. It is not my intent to add significantly to the growing base of human resources theories and models, although a few models will be offered. Instead, this is one person's story that can act as a reference point for those who are working desperately to figure out how to make the transition to a more strategic role. It is the story that I looked for fifteen years ago, but could not find.

My insight comes from real experience, having been a VP-HR in three major companies in three different industries. I am not an academic, and I am not a longtime consultant. I have worked inside companies for 25 years. I have written this book as someone who has experimented, who has taken risks to pioneer a new approach. Many of those risks have worked exactly as I had hoped. Some of them proved to be ill-founded. Some of them proved to be very costly personally. All increased my understanding of how to transform an HR group into true business partners who focus on the marketplace and connect human resources work to business strategy.

This book is not for someone looking for absolute direction in every area of strategic human resources. It is for the HR professional who is creative enough in his or her own thinking to take a real example of strategic human resources in practice, consider it, take it apart, and put it back together again, perhaps somewhat differently. I do not attempt to offer the perfect answer for every organization. The field is still in the midst of significant change. Frankly, I hope I raise as many questions as I offer answers. But in this emerging field, many of the questions have not yet been asked. And for me, that is precisely what makes it such an interesting arena in which to work.

Roadmap to Strategic HR

CHAPTER ONE

The Complexity of the Challenge

PERHAPS THERE HAS NEVER BEEN a more challenging time for business leaders. The stock market is being ravaged by forces previously unconsidered. Terrorist attacks have specifically targeted the disruption of Western business as part of a war plan. Executives have been exposed for engaging in clearly unethical management practices aimed at lining their own pockets at the expense of investors, employees, and retirees. Investor confidence runs hot and cold. Consumers are nervous. Social and business values around the world are changing dramatically, making it increasingly challenging to predict the consumer, workforce, and business environment of the future.

Many business leaders are desperately searching for an edge in this ever more competitive environment. Cautious about using financial "tricks" as the solution, and seemingly unable to gain the advantage with product design or marketing alone, more and more of these leaders are considering how they manage their human and organizational resources as the answer.

Multiple factors have produced this incredibly complex context for business in general and for human resources specifically. Some of them are discussed here.

Globalization

Globalization, which has been alluded to for years, is now much more of a reality. While its benefits are clear in terms of the new markets it opens, many business leaders are unprepared to deal with the significant set of challenges it brings. Highly paid Western workers cannot compete with lower-paid but similarly skilled overseas workers.

Technology has made this an even more acute problem in the United States. There is a great deal of high-cost technology work that can begin in the United States on one day, be sent overseas to be completed overnight, and returned the next day at a fraction of the cost. Examples in my experience include:

- An engineering team that begins a project on one continent, then simply ships it electronically around the world at the end of the workday to an engineering team just starting the day on another continent. This allows the company to have twenty-four hours of progress each day on engineering projects. Think of the implications of this form of work for an industry that is highly conscious of time-to-market or cost of design.

- Accounting, technical support, or other routine efforts that can be outsourced to lower-cost countries.

The cost of global shipping and communications has dropped drastically over the past fifty years. As a result, labor rates more and more are becoming a primary differentiator in global competitiveness. This places a growing number of American workers in a less competitive and increasingly powerless position. The ratio of entry-level wage earners to retirees is expected to drop from 9 to 1 in 1955 to 2 to 1 in 2020.[1]

The War for Top Talent

The war for top talent continues to intensify. While the number of college-educated employees is increasing in the United States, this does not equal a surplus of talent. Some believe that on average American talent is becoming less competitive with other global talent pools. Top students have lots of options and are demanding the ability to have more challenging work and career opportunities. They are looking for work that is more likely to significantly advance their career and earning power.

The Increasing Pressure on Employees

It is not only leaders but also today's employee who is under pressure never before experienced. Technology has made it not only possible but in many industries a requirement that employees work far longer hours than in the past. People are taking more work home with them. The idea of retirement is being drastically redefined. Baby boomers who had dreamed of an early retirement are feeling pressed into working longer than expected, often in jobs that they never intended to take. Many will likely work as long as their health permits.

The American economy is undergoing a significant transition from a predominantly product-focused economy to one with an increasing focus on services. Some predict that service workers will represent 88 percent of the American workforce by 2025. This is having, and will continue to have, a drastic impact upon the workforce. Employees are terrified as they see jobs requiring their skills moving offshore while they have little perceived ability to build the skills needed for the jobs that will stay. They feel betrayed by employers and politicians and are becoming increasingly and understandably angry. These issues impact the mood and productivity inside organizations and cannot be ignored by human resources professionals.

The Continuing Decline in Employee Loyalty

Fewer employees feel a sense of loyalty and commitment to a given company, as they feel that loyalty is rarely reciprocated. Though many

may view this trend as inevitable, and some may even view it posi-
tively, this loss of loyalty between employee and company undoubtedly
has its disadvantages. Some companies are attempting to engender a
stronger sense of employee commitment by acknowledging and supporting employee loyalty to their industry or technology, rather than
loyalty only to the company. While many are gambling that this will
help, nobody knows the long-term implications of such a shift in
thinking about employee loyalty.

The Ongoing Decline in Customer Loyalty

Customers are becoming increasingly demanding of their suppliers.
As one author says, "The starkest challenge facing business today is
customer scarcity: too many sellers for too few buyers. There is simply
too much of everything for customers to absorb. In just a few years,
customers in nearly every field have metamorphosed from dependable, pliant shoppers to elusive, picky know-it-alls who tell you precisely what they want, how and when they want it, and how much they
will pay for it. And if for some reason you are unable to gratify them,
off they go to find someone who will."[2] Long-term relationships and
customer loyalty are dissolving as customers assert their right to take
their business elsewhere as other suppliers offer better-value proposi-
tions.

Having an organizational culture where all employees understand
how their work impacts the customer has never been more important.
And yet this is an incredibly difficult change initiative to pull off successfully.

The Strenuous Intervention of Shareholders and Boards of Directors

Shareholders and boards of directors are becoming increasingly demanding of management. They have moved into much more active

roles in maintaining company value. They are less and less willing to put up with management that does not perform or that performs outside the bounds of established ethics. These issues impact who is hired and the development processes that need to occur.

The Increased Speed of Change

Nearly every organization is struggling to deal with the increasing rate of change in our complex global industries and companies. As more information becomes immediately available from dispersed operations, decisions are made in real time, sending a variety of change messages and expectations into the organization. It is ever more difficult to keep track of the "whole system." As a result, the coordination of varied change efforts becomes more and more challenging. This change atmosphere is often confusing and overwhelming, particularly for lower-level managers and employees.

Human issues by their nature tend to be complex issues. Now put them in the context of these incredibly challenging conditions in the business environment, and the need for skilled HR leaders has never been greater.

Are HR Leaders Up to the Challenge?

Unfortunately, too few HR professionals have developed the business skills, combined with more sophisticated human resources domain skills, to add the needed value to these complex business issues. I had the opportunity recently to listen to a large group of senior HR leaders openly discuss their perceptions of why they are not accepted at the business table. Their points included these problems:

- They spend too much time discussing the details of human resources stuff that doesn't appear to relate to the issues of the business.

- They seek line management's direction and leadership and don't think often enough about providing that leadership themselves.
- They lack the detailed business knowledge that allows them to talk intelligently about the business issues. They don't understand the customers, the technology, the industry, the competitors, the channels, and so on.
- They don't tie human resources initiatives to the bottom line well enough.
- They use a unique language that doesn't appeal to the employee or management.
- They don't bring enough to the strategic conversation. They move too quickly to the details of execution.
- They haven't helped others at the business table understand either through concept or experiences why HR is at the table.

Now clearly there are an increasing number of examples where we find HR leaders who have learned to overcome most or all of these issues. However, many have yet to do so. This was a very sophisticated HR group, and its members clearly saw that they still made many traditional mistakes.

This same group of global HR leaders recently assessed its own readiness and its colleagues' readiness to meet these strategic demands. On average, the group members said that well over half simply cannot meet these demands. This is both great news and terrible news. This is great news for the HR professional who is strategic and who can make the connections among customer requirements, business strategies, and human resources responses. But this is bad news for the CEO who needs talented HR leadership to step up today.

Distinguishing Between Tactical and Strategic Human Resources

Paul McKinnon, currently SVP-HR at Dell, had been with the company only a short time when a senior executive asked him how many employees there were in the organization. He was unable to give a precise answer. This may sound to some like it should be an easy question. All of us who have sat in the top HR role know how complex this question actually is, depending upon who is counted and who is not counted. (Are we talking about head count or FTEs? Do we include contractors? Consultants? And so on.) So McKinnon didn't feel confident giving a definitive answer to the question.

Some time later, this same executive asked McKinnon if he knew how many employees there were in the company. Once again, McKinnon admitted that he couldn't give a precise answer that would line up with everyone else's numbers. The executive responded thoughtfully, "If I can't trust you to count, how can I trust you with anything important?" This executive highlighted how HR professionals must demonstrate competency in the tactics to earn trust on strategic issues.

McKinnon reminds us that "Even after we get the operational aspects of human resources working well, we have to keep earning that trust every day. If it ever falls off, we will automatically and immediately lose license to work on the more strategic elements of human resources work." He continues, "Human resources work starts and ends with operational excellence. The distinction between operational and strategic human resources work becomes blurred. Most human resources work that we do has aspects of both."

Understanding Terms: HR and hr

Perhaps before defining more clearly what I mean by strategic human resources, I should point out a distinction that I make between human resources and HR. I will be using both terms; we all do. The problem is that we often use them interchangeably when they are in fact very different. When I refer to human resources, I am talking about work that deals with people and organizations. It has nothing necessarily to do with the HR department or HR professionals. It is about the work. People work.

It is important to remember that human resources work is done whether or not the company has any type of HR organization or group. HR is an investment in resources to help the organization do human resources work. Business leaders choose to invest in an HR department because they need technical help in the arena of people management. They should not invest in an HR department so that someone else can do all of the people aspects of their work. Instead, the HR department should enable managers to better fulfill their responsibilities in managing people.

Defining Tactical and Strategic Human Resources

Now let's define the work. What do I mean by tactical human resources? What is strategic human resources? Paul McKinnon's experience at Dell shows us that we can't fall into the trap of assuming that one is important and the other is unimportant, that one adds value and the other does not. Nothing could be further from the truth. They are both important. They simply are very different.

Part of this problem comes from language used in many work and organization redesign efforts. Many organizational consultants have large HR groups distinguish between different types of human resources work. They do this so that they can differentiate the work as part of their design effort. Unfortunately, the administrative work is often categorized as "routine," "nonessential," "noncritical," or "work not linked to competitive advantage," while the more strategic elements are elegantly named "value-added" or "competitive" work. While it may or may not be intended, the implications are clear—one set is important, and the other is not.

We are in dangerous territory if we succumb to talking about strategic elements of HR as being important and others as not important. We are, however, in equally dangerous territory if we are unable to distinguish the differences between strategic and tactical/administrative work. They are different. While both types of work need to be done well, strategic human resources work is much more directly connected to the company's strategy and its implementation. They require very different skills. And they clearly contribute to the strategic differentiation in the marketplace to vastly different degrees.

Tactical Human Resources

When speaking of tactical human resources, I tend to refer to:

- Baseline administration of people issues and data. Examples include:
  - Benefits administration
  - Compensation administration
  - Employee records
  - Affirmative action reporting
  - Policy development and enforcement
- Implementation of traditional human resources programs and work
  - Hiring
  - Basic skills training
  - Salary surveys and compensation program design
  - Employee relations work of resolving day-to-day employee concerns and problems

These are the more traditional activities for which HR is known. HR has been about this work for many years. These are valuable activities. It will always be important to do fundamental human resources administration well. It really does matter to people whether or not they receive a paycheck on time!

But, in delivering tactical human resources, it is quite possible to fulfill the work exactly as required without realizing that it may be the wrong work, work that is no longer needed, or work that in fact now gets in the way of what the organization is trying to accomplish. Success in tactical human resources is generally measured by one's ability to accomplish a predefined activity competently. Far too infrequently do we pause to ask if it is still the right work or if it is being done in the right way. It is instead quite easy to fall into a routine of doing things in a particular way because we can do them that way, because we have built the skills to do them in a certain way. There is a huge difference between doing what is right and needed and doing what we know how to do.

Human Resources Administration Costs and Competitive Advantage

Important as they are, the tactics of human resources do not generally give an organization competitive advantage. They don't tend to differentiate the entity from its competitors. I recently spoke with a colleague who had left a major HR consulting firm. This firm did a wonderful job at redesigning specific human resources processes for efficiency and cost reductions. But, as he pointed out, this work does not distinguish a company from the pack. Everyone is looking at outsourcing. Everyone is exploring the role of shared services. Everyone is utilizing technology. Everyone is cutting human resources costs. These pursuits have become the cost of admission in the game. They simply allow one to play. They don't differentiate.

My colleague and I agreed that it is the nuances of strategic human resources that differentiate a company in the marketplace. Strategies to recognize how talent can be leveraged to deliver on customer needs differentiate a business. Generally, efficiency does not. Differentiation is more about partnering and gaining the trust and respect of line management and employees than it is about cost cutting and efficient administration.

My friend eventually left the consulting firm because its leadership seemed unable to understand that the customer was looking for more than the firm was then able to provide. Rather than learning how to provide new offerings, which would have brought in new and very profitable consulting business, it continued to do what it had done for years, in the same way that it had done business. Among other losses, it lost a very talented person who demanded to be part of a firm that was focused on what the customer needed, rather than what the firm could provide easily.

Strategic Human Resources

The move to strategic human resources assumes that administrative competence in needed areas is a given. Again, one never gets the invitation to be strategic if the appropriate administrative basics are not in place and functioning like clockwork. Strategic human resources work focuses on the path between human talent and winning in the marketplace. It looks at the relationships among the human, financial, market, and technological assets of an organization in order to build organizational capabilities that enable companies to win in the marketplace. Examples of strategic human resources efforts might include:

- Stimulating dialogue among the executive team to reexamine the clarity and/or appropriateness of business strategy

- Aligning reward systems across the organization to ensure that they consistently encourage the fulfillment of customer needs

- Reassessing and projecting talent needs on the basis of the latest business strategies

- Redesigning work processes to eliminate aspects that don't add value or that unnecessarily increase cost for the end consumer

- Developing training solutions to build organizational capabilities required by the business strategy

- Redesigning aspects of the organizational culture that inhibit the delivery of what the customer desires in the way of speed, creativity, quality, service levels, or whatever needs improvement

These are simply a few examples. Over the course of this book, I will offer a much more in-depth picture of what strategic human resources work looks like. But the major differentiator is that this work connects to building competitive advantage, to enabling business strategy, to fulfilling customer needs.

Strategic Human Resources Work and Its Connection to the Customer

Many people struggle to make a conceptual connection between HR professionals and the customer. But strategic human resources work is fundamentally based on business strategy that is (or should be) connected to satisfying customer needs. Let me give an example where I, as an HR professional, was literally involved with the customer.

While I worked at DEC, our sales group was actively pursuing significant business with a large bank in New York City. We continued to find that we were competitive at the product sell, but we couldn't differentiate DEC through product alone. The salespeople needed something to differentiate us from other strong system providers.

I knew one of the key technical architects on the sales team well. He asked me if I had any thoughts on how we might differentiate DEC in the selling process. I talked with him about the customer's stated problem, which involved networking computer systems between their central headquarters in New York and out-of-state branches from a recent acquisition. I framed the customer's need in organizational terms, rather than technical terms. I told my technical colleague that his product technology was simply the means to an end. What the company really needed was to design a communications and control process between the subsidiary branches and corporate.

I had the same conversation with the sales team, and it was pleased with the new framing of the customer need. The members liked it because it was put in terms that the customer would recognize. I was invited to the customer headquarters in the next scheduled meeting and led the conversation about framing DEC's response to the customer's needs in organizational, rather than purely technical, terms. The customer was delighted and could now see that DEC brought something new that in fact differentiated our proposal.

Not all of our customer influence in HR can be quite that direct. Probably the most common way for HR to satisfy customer needs occurs when HR designs the internal systems that allow the company to meet and exceed the customer's expectations of the company. These may be talent systems, training systems, rewards systems that incent behaviors the customer values, or work processes that improve the interaction for the customer and reduce costs for the customer. This is strategic human resources. It is work that ultimately makes a difference to the end customer, as well as to the company's ability to meet its strategy.

Why the Customer Connection Is Vital

Some may ask why it is not enough to say that human resources work helps the company meet its strategy. Why does it have to be connected to the customer? It may not need to be connected to the customer if every company strategy is perfectly aligned with the needs of the customer. But the truth is that they rarely are.

If human resources work is solely focused on the internal strategy and the internal strategy misses the mark, an effective HR group will ironically help the company miss the customer needs better and faster. HR must be focused on customer needs and become a voice that ensures that all internal activity is focused on meeting those needs. HR may be the only internal voice that is able or willing to push management to reexamine if it really knows the customer needs. I discuss this in greater detail in Chapter 7. Too often, management that has done business successfully in a certain way for years is blind to the fact that the customer has changed course and is looking for a new response. HR must be able to tell the emperor that he has no clothes and help him to get refocused.

This is the type of human resources work that directly connects to the success of the business. It goes beyond administration to address larger competitive and organizational questions. HR professionals who can engage well at this level of complexity earn the trust of their line leaders and the right to sit at the table as strategic business partners.

Notes

1. Richard W. Judy and Carol D'Amico, *Workforce 2020: Work and Workers in the 21st Century* (Indianapolis: Hudson Institute, 1999).

2. Fred Wiersema, *The New Market Leaders: Who's Winning and How in the Battle for Customers* (New York: Free Press, 2001), pp. 45–46.

CHAPTER TWO

From Rigid Administrators to Strategic Contributors

MOST OF US HAVE EXPERIENCED a personnel or HR department that seemed overwhelmed in paperwork or details. Some of these departments are almost comical displays of bureaucratic inefficiencies. Many of us have interacted with an HR representative who seemed absolutely inflexible and unable to consider any possibility that wasn't "by the book." Personnel/HR groups historically established a reputation that they still battle today.

The Evolution of HR

It might be helpful to put strategic human resources into a historical context that shows what it is and how the field has evolved over time. Strategic human resources work is relatively new in the history of personnel or HR groups. Like most fields, the function of HR has evolved through the decades, influenced by both internal learnings and external trends and theories. Through this evolution, HR has passed through a series of stages. Each of the stages listed in Figure 2-1 is descriptive of many organizations' current HR reality, regardless of what the function is currently called.

Figure 2-1. HR stages of development.

Function Usually Known As:	Primary Focus	Talent Background
Purchasing	Hiring and firing at best costs.	Contract negotiations; little focus on human sensitivity.
Labor Relations	Negotiating with unions representing company employees; negotiating talent for least costs.	Legal and negotiating background.
Personnel	Administering employee issues such as benefits, compensation, and employee relations; tends to have a strong emphasis on control.	Administrative background.
Human Resources (HR)	In many cases, represents primarily a name change with little substantive difference, regardless of the implication of a move toward being more strategic.	Both administrative and employee relations background; increasing focus on business processes.
Strategic HR	Managing organization and employee performance.	Background in business strategy, people, systems, and organization.

In the beginnings of modern business, the staffing function was essentially one more line item on the list for Purchasing. It acquired and got rid of people. People were viewed and treated much like one more commodity to be bought and sold at the best price. There was virtually no attention paid to sensitivity to people's needs or to their productivity. Productivity was left entirely to management.

The field of personnel had evolved by the 1950s and 1960s and even into the 1970s into a function that focused primarily on hiring, compensation/benefits administration, labor relations/union management, and employee relations. Many of the leaders in personnel came up through compensation/benefits or labor relations. While these were—and continue to be—very important areas of work to be accomplished, they were not viewed as integral components of managing the strategic elements of the business. They were administrative necessities with which management typically wanted little involvement. Personnel's job was primarily to make sure that employee problems and costs were kept to a minimum and that talent was available when and where it was needed.

With a growing awareness of individual employee needs and an assumption that a happy and engaged worker is a more productive worker, the personnel department in many companies strengthened its employee relations focus and renamed its group "Human Resources." Though the title suggests looking at people as a critical asset to be leveraged in the creation of value, most departments remained highly administrative, and, in most cases, there was more focus on protecting employees than on leveraging their skills to enable business strategy.

The Relationship Between Organization Development and HR

In the late 1960s and early 1970s, a new field emerged out of the social psychology arena. This new discipline became known as organizational behavior or organization development (OD). Initially, it tended to focus on the effectiveness of individuals and small teams. In its early years, this emerging field was distinct and separate from the personnel/HR functions of that time. Over time, OD became part of many personnel/HR groups, but the two fields had an odd, almost tense relationship. Those involved in classic human resources administration were often uncomfortable with many of the basic premises of the new field of organization development. They and their line management counterparts had a sense for its potential, but they were often suspicious and somewhat envious of the newfound interest that management evinced in OD groups.

Through the 1970s, it became clear to leaders in the field that focus on individuals and small team behavior/effectiveness, while interesting, was not enough. Through the mid-1970s, an increasing amount of attention was given to the implication of organizational processes and systems for the behavior of individuals and small groups. People in OD began looking much more closely at these elements:

- Planning systems

- Measurement systems

- Organizational structure and corporate governance

- Work flows as a system

- Budgeting and economics as a system

They began to realize that all of these organizational systems had to work together if they were to have a significant impact on human behavior.

However, as the field of organization development evolved, it remained quite separate from the personnel groups of the day. Most people in OD wanted nothing to do with what they viewed as bureaucratic personnel departments or the emerging Human Resources function. While some OD groups were structured as part of HR, many were not. When the two functions were joined structurally, far too often they still remained distinct in terms of the work to be done.

OD often worked hard to establish an identity separate from HR. Some organizations literally created two separate structures—one for personnel/HR and another for OD. When OD and HR were structured separately, this seemed to ensure that HR remained administrative and bureaucratic. At the same time, most people in personnel or HR wanted little to do with the emerging field of organization development. Many saw it as "pie in the sky," as not being grounded in reality, as being far too risky a venture to propose to their line leadership.

Despite this gap between OD and HR, the discipline of organization development was key in the evolution of strategic human resources. From organization development came the approach of connecting daily work to the development and fulfillment of organizational strategy. The organization development discipline has strengthened and enhanced many other areas of human resources.

Let me be clear that strategic human resources is not a "takeover" of HR by the OD crowd. Some have made the mistake of viewing it as such. Organization development as a discipline is not the new criterion for HR leadership. Rather, the new HR leaders need to be strategic and systemic in their thinking and diagnostics. I would argue that, in the recent past, OD has proved to develop these strategic skills faster and better than most other groups in HR. By its nature, organization development is strategic. By its nature, it is about the design of systems that support the overall vision and purpose of the organization. These qualities give an HR leader the ability to approach her work in a much more strategic manner. HR leadership does not, however, require a formal organization development background. It absolutely does require a strategic/systemic background. Many current successful leaders of strategic HR groups have some organization development experience in their background.

The Evolution of the Way I Viewed HR

After finishing graduate school, I spent my first eight years as an internal OD consultant first at Digital Equipment Corporation and then at Martin Marietta. I will never forget the utter shock I felt when Peter Koch, a senior HR leader at Digital, asked me to come directly from graduate school into a personnel job. He argued that this was critical in transforming what was called personnel into a truly strategic force in the company. He also tried to convince me that it was in my long-term best interest and that this was surely the direction that the field was going.

I couldn't conceive any value in such a job selection. Why in the world would I waste a great academic background in organization development by moving into personnel? It would be many years before I realized how insightful Peter Koch had been. He was probably way ahead of his time with his vision of transforming the personnel or HR function by combining it with organization development theory and skills. But, because of my obstinacy, Peter patiently allowed me to move directly into an OD job that I truly loved.

After spending about eight years in internal OD consulting roles, I was once again invited to think seriously about a move into HR leadership. Frankly, I wanted no part of it. I still considered much of the work done by HR to be cumbersome, bureaucratic, and administrative. I did not see it as being strategic in nature, nor did I see it as being able to take advantage of the strategic and systems skills that I believed I had developed as an OD professional.

However, my systems thinking eventually got the best of me. I began to realize that if I was serious about organization effectiveness, I had to become serious about key human resource systems. For example, I had to become serious about the process of rewarding and acknowledging behavior. If I was serious about organization effectiveness, I had to become serious about the process of acquiring and retaining talent and planning for future talent. If I was serious about organizational effectiveness, I had to become serious abut the training and development processes of employees.

In essence, I began to realize that anyone who is serious about organization effectiveness has to be equally serious about all of the components of human resource management. The problem was not that human resource management was unimportant or irrelevant. The problem was that throughout the 1970s and 1980s it was not being managed in a very strategic manner. But most OD professionals wanted nothing to do with HR.

Conversely, my friends in HR who were thoughtful about their field had to realize that if they were serious about people—even if their primary interest was the treatment of people—they had to be serious about the design of organizations and the design of work. They had to be serious about the role that organization and work flow played in the experience of employees from day to day. They had to be serious about management processes and systems. These systems had as much influence upon the experience and feelings of the employee as anything else could. Yet most HR professionals wanted nothing to do with OD.

I realized that the serious OD person and the serious HR person had to understand that while there were aspects of each of these separate fields that needed to be fixed, these fields were conceptually joined at the hip. The field simply needed leadership that could begin to see the interdependence of the two fields and the points of overlap with the field of strategy. It needed leadership that could help meld the three into one common field that had the best interests of people and of organizations at heart. It needed more people like Peter Koch.

I was delighted some years later when colleagues in the Organizational Behavior Department of Brigham Young University developed a simple model (Figure 2-2) that legitimized the relationship between these three disciplines. This simple yet elegant depiction illustrates the emerging field I was facing and has come to guide my conceptual framework for strategic human resources. I made my first foray into

Figure 2-2. Model of relationship among HR strategies.

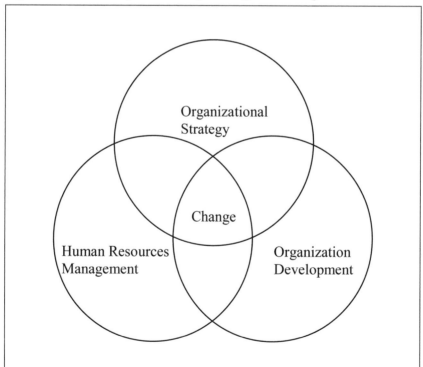

human resources with a clear vision: to connect the strategic components of organizational behavior with the critical human resources components, which I still did not understand terribly well at that point.

The first thing that I did as a budding HR practitioner in the mid-1980s was to seek out the experts in this emerging field of strategic human resources. Unfortunately, in those early days, I found too few HR practitioners who had developed the business sense, strategic perspective, and system thinking skills needed to add value to complex business issues. The majority of the HR leaders with whom I had associated had grown up in the administrative or labor relations sides of human resources and had not made the strategic connection to the business.

I did, however, find a group of academics and consultants who were beginning to bring the two fields of human resources and organization development together conceptually. (See the Appendix for recommended articles and books by some of the clearest theorists on strategic human resources.) They spoke eloquently of the need for HR leaders who contribute to business strategy development, who are agents of change and organizational productivity and also champions of the employee.

HR in Our Decade

Over the past decade, the field of HR has gone through unprecedented change. This change has been fueled by the creative thinking and writing of an emerging cadre of academics and consultants, including Ed Schein, Ed Lawler, Dave Ulrich, Norm Smallwood, Wayne Brockbank, Jac Fitz-enz, Michael Losey, and Gerry Lake. They have been incredibly helpful in expanding the way that HR professionals and line management think about HR. Their contributions have included:

- Making a compelling case for a new human resources.

- Providing clarity around the different roles that HR professionals might play. Ulrich describes these roles as:
  - Strategic partner
  - Administrative expert
  - Employee champion
  - Change agent[1]

- Identifying the competencies that are needed in each of these areas. As a result, a rapidly growing number of HR professionals have started the process of developing these competencies.

- Offering new insights into the measurement of human resources results and suggesting how to know if HR is making any real difference.

- Creating the concept of business partnership, the need to connect with the business and make a difference on bottom-line results.

All of these contributions have moved the human resources field forward significantly.

Another tremendous contribution is found in the book *Why The Bottom Line ISN'T.* In this volume, Ulrich and Smallwood summarize a landmark piece of research by Baruch Lev of New York University. Lev makes the case that, while historically there was a high correlation between hard assets and the stock price of a company, over recent years the hard assets of a company seem to account for significantly less of the stock price or value of the company. Lev explores what accounts for the rest of a company's valuation. He describes the other critical factors as "intangibles."

Ulrich and Smallwood explain, "Lev has defined the intangibles from a financial perspective as a claim to future benefits that does not have a physical or financial (stock or bond) embodiment. He further identified sources of intangibles as discovery, organization, and human resources . . . human resource intangibles focus on training, culture, and leadership. Lev further suggests that the human resources domain of intangibles requires more work."[2] It appears there is a direct connection between effective human resources work and organizational value. The quality of our attention to organization, leadership, and culture has a real connection to a company's value.

Ulrich and Smallwood quote Robert Eccles and his colleagues at PricewaterhouseCoopers, who indicated that "Only 19 percent of investors and 27 percent of analysts 'found financial reports very useful in communicating the true value of companies.' They found three clusters of performance indicators that mattered most:

1. Customers: Sales and marketing costs, distribution challenges, brand equity, and customer turnover rates

2. Employees: intellectual capital, employee retention, and revenue per employee

3. Innovation: revenues from new products, new product success rate, R&D expenditures, and product development cycle."[3]

What a remarkable case for the need to focus on human resources work. The overall value of the entity is in significant measure created by the effective management of the human resources of the organization. This assessment isn't put forth from a big HR professional organization—it's coming from financial analysts. The business case is real. The human factor of an organization and how effectively it is managed make a significant difference to the financial success of the enterprise.

Such contributions have been invaluable. They have stretched the minds of those interested in human resources work and encouraged them to explore new ways to think about their field. However, many practitioners are still struggling to learn how to implement these new concepts.

Many HR Leaders Want to Be Strategic Partners But Aren't Sure How

Why haven't more HR leaders developed the skills to become more influential, more sought-after business partners? Quite honestly, I don't know the entire answer. I suspect that there are many reasons. I am convinced that most would like to be strong business partners. Some may have come into the field specifically because they had not succeeded in leading significant pieces of the business. For some, it became a politically "safe" place to wait for retirement. Some may simply have lacked the interest or aptitude to develop needed business and strategic skills. Still others have not heard line leaders asking for more than administration and therefore never thought to offer it up. These leaders have done exactly what they have been rewarded for many years for doing.

However, I believe that the majority of HR leaders have enough desire and enough basic aptitude to be influential business partners. Most who struggle today in making the transition to being strategic business partners lack an understanding of how to translate great human resources theory into tangible applications. They lack the vision to illustrate for their line counterparts the partnership they can provide. They lack the language with which to talk about the connection between people issues and business success. They lack tools and approaches to make the theory real. And they may also lack the confidence to bring it all together. While characteristics such as confidence may be difficult to develop, I believe that as HR professionals become more strategic and skilled, they will exhibit greater confidence as they have more meaningful influence upon the organization.

Translating Theory into Real Applications

My personal frustration has been that as I have looked at the emerging theory base of strategic human resources, I haven't found enough cases where it has been implemented. In fact, I have come to believe that one of the problems with the field is that the theory has out-stripped the practice. We need many more stories of leaders who have taken the risk to try the theory and have found what works and what doesn't. We need internal HR leaders who are strong conceptually and able to envision the application of the theory base. As a result, I and many others have come to find that our practitioner roles make us pioneers of sorts in the field of strategic human resources as we take great theories and concepts and try to learn how to implement them in the realities of large, complex organizations.

A Theory Isn't Worth Much if It Breaks Down in Practice

My father was a research metallurgical engineer. I recall his taking me as a young boy into his research labs, where he worked hard on new theories regarding the strength of welded steel. He was obsessed with finding ways to make welds stronger. He collected tremendous amounts of data and analyzed them endlessly. He postulated what was needed to create a better weld. But all of that research really meant very little until he left his research lab and walked into the dirty, smelly welding shop to see if any of the theory actually worked. Sometimes it did, and sometimes it didn't. When it didn't, he went back to the theoretical research with learnings from the test welds he had just done and applied the new insights to his growing body of understanding.

This same iterative learning process exists in most fields; it certainly exists in the field of human resources. The past three decades have produced a growing pool of exciting theory about strategic human resources—the value HR can add to an organization and the role that "business partners" can play. But much of human resources theory is untested and unproven. It often makes assumptions that work well in the ideal world but start to break down in practice. What has been largely missing is that iterative process of testing the theory, learning from experimentation, and revising the theory to then test it again. And after garnering these learnings, we have lacked methods to share these learnings more broadly among HR practitioners.

The basics are coming together, but there is much work yet to be done. That is part of what makes this a great field to enter. It is an exciting time not only for academics and consultants but particularly for the HR practitioners who are actually trying to make it happen in big organizations.

Foundation for My Insights

In this book, I offer the perspective of one who has been applying sound human resource theories in the messy lab of real organizations. My knowledge is based on twenty-five years of working inside organizations, from the sometimes uncomfortable position of watching theory break down in practice. I share some experiments that were tremendously successful and some that were disappointments. Understanding what went wrong and how to do things differently next time has given me some of my greatest learnings about transforming an HR organization.

Most of these efforts were attempted as I led an HR organization, which I did as a VP-HR in three major companies in three different industries. My most recent experience as a VP-HR was at Hallmark Cards, Inc., where I inherited a strong but rather traditional HR group. In this book, I draw most heavily on my Hallmark experience. When I left Hallmark, I believe it had one of the most strategic HR groups in industry.

How can I claim that these approaches actually made a difference? Always believing that the only real measure for HR is a positive change in business results, I compared business results at Hallmark from the five years before we transformed the HR organization to the five years after the changes in HR were implemented. The business results showed significant and measurable increases in ROAM, operating profit, net shipments, market share, and, ultimately, profit sharing for employees.

Clearly, all of these results did not come solely as a result of discrete HR efforts. However, the CEO and I both agreed that key HR efforts were critical, in conjunction with other important initiatives, to generate these results. I am quite convinced that these systems would never have been designed and implemented were it not for a significantly different approach taken to human resources work. These results suggest to me that thoughtful work on the people side of the business can have measurable impact upon the outcomes of the organization.

Roadmap to Strategic HR

So what are the components to transitioning HR from an administrative function—at times considered irrelevant—to a function that makes a real difference to business results? On the basis of my experience, I have developed a particular approach to transforming an HR organization. I believe that the following components create the roadmap to make the transition:

1. Assess the organization's readiness for change.

2. Develop and institutionalize a framework and language for human resources.

3. Understand the senior HR leader's role as organizational architect.

4. Clarify line management's role and engage top management in creating and owning human resources strategy.

5. Create a human and organizational plan (HRP).

6. Understand the five human resources processes through a strategic lens.

7. Clarify the roles of generalist and specialist.

8. Design the structure of your new HR organization.

9. Assess and upgrade your HR talent.

10. Recognize the roadblocks and political land mines in making the transition to strategic HR.

It is tempting to think about these ten components as linear occurrences, to assume that you start with Step 1 and proceed in sequence through Step 10. I don't view them quite that narrowly. Frankly, they must be rolled out in a much more integrated and systemic fashion. I suspect that each organization's circumstances and needs will require a somewhat unique and different approach. But I do believe that all ten components are important and interconnected.

Despite that caveat about not being overly structured, I do believe that a few of these steps should be done in sequence. For example, I believe that you really should start with the assessment of readiness, followed by the development of a framework. The assessment gives you a baseline from which to work. The framework gives you a language with which to talk about what you are doing. I would not attempt a change in HR without first paying attention to these two components.

I would also be keenly aware of the political roadblocks that you are likely to encounter and be thoughtful early on in the process about how you will deal with them. They are deadly. They can make or break a change effort. You will get great insights into the political issues as you do the assessment.

The other components have to do with roles and structure leading to the eventual development of the HR Plan. I wouldn't feel that I had to have everything in place before taking a first cut at the HR Plan. As soon as line management was engaged, I would probably take a first cut at the HR Plan. I would not, however, do it without having line management engaged. Engaging line management is perhaps the most commonly ignored component of the process, but in many ways it is the whole point of strategic human resources.

The chapters of this book deal with each of the components I have mentioned. Each chapter provides illustrations, thought-provoking questions, tools, and frameworks for implementing each component. I suggest that the reader go through the chapters in this book in the order that they appear, but be prepared to develop your particular plan in a sequence that best meets the needs outlined by your assessment.

Notes

1. Dave Ulrich, *Human Resource Champions* (Boston: Harvard Business School Press, 1997).

2. Dave Ulrich and Norm Smallwood, *Why the Bottom Line ISN'T!: How to Build Value Through People and Organization* (New York: Wiley, 2003), p. 7.

3. Ibid., p.8.

CHAPTER THREE

Assess the Organization's Readiness for Change

BEFORE YOU CAN GET ANYWHERE in changing a company's HR focus from an administrative to a strategic approach, you need to know whether the company is truly open to change. One company I worked with had a new head of HR with a strategic background who requested that I come in and help in the transformation to a more strategic HR organization. I was delighted. We were optimistic about our chances of making change. Unfortunately, neither the new head of HR nor I realized at first that the CEO and key members of the executive team were very tactical, internally focused, and reluctant to change. On the one hand, these executives mouthed their desire for change and influence from HR, and yet in much of what they did they declared their deeper desire to keep things very much the same. As a result, the changes were slow and painful to realize.

This is only one example of the need to do an initial assessment of the organization's readiness to change. Such an assessment, taken seriously, will help tremendously in how you design your change plan. One potential obstacle may be a lack of management support, as I just described. Another may have to do with the readiness of HR leadership or the depth of HR talent. Yet another may have to do with influences in the marketplace that impact how the company will approach its change. In any event, do not forgo this assessment component as you prepare to transform your HR organization to a strategic one.

Some climates are not yet conducive to developing a strategic HR focus. Many line and HR leaders read the theory and have a quick reaction that it is exactly what they need and want to do. While the desire to change is important, it is not enough to make the change happen.

In Chapter 2, I outlined the development of the human resources field and described some common turf wars between groups. A wide range of roles and expectations exists for HR departments in various organizations. While certain HR departments may be completely focused on administration and processes within HR, others may have developed a focus on the business and the marketplace. The stage of the HR department and the cultural and political conditions of the organization are extremely important to recognize in order to lead a successful change effort. Each organization has its own unique set of factors—factors that require that you take a particular path as you attempt to change its approach to HR.

Some business leaders have naively announced that HR has or will be transformed without making any significant change in line leadership's views or increasing strategic human resources skills in the organization. Other leaders have announced a change without having the HR talent in place that is capable of actually behaving differently. These and other false starts have the ability to render any true long-term change nearly impossible.

That's why assessing the organization's readiness for change should be done before considerable investment is made. At a minimum, this assessment phase will be instructive regarding the most effective approaches for change to take for that particular organization. The assessment may even suggest that now is not the right time to make the attempt.

Questions to Ask to Determine Organizational Readiness

The following eleven questions may help you to gain a preliminary perspective on HR in your organization. Management and HR professionals should pose these questions thoughtfully as they assess the current state of HR and begin to identify opportunities for improvement.

1. *How valued is HR in our organization? What is its reputation? How strategic is it?*

Though the answer may not be flattering, it's important to be frank about this. What is the real reputation? I remember that when I first came to Hallmark, management was very clear that it was looking for a new approach to HR. Though individual HR professionals were highly valued and trusted by line leaders, the group as a whole had a reputation for often being bogged down in administration and bureaucracy. Many managers felt that HR seemed more intent on driving its own agenda than on focusing on the needs of the business. Leaders were also concerned that too many HR initiatives seemed totally disconnected from one another.

In contrast to the reputation I just described, I know of many organizations in Hallmark now that will not have key business meetings without trusted HR leaders there because they know that when HR is in attendance the quality of the meetings improves. HR professionals consistently raise questions that help move the vision of the organization along.

2. *How does our human resources work align with and support the strategy of the organization?*

A very telling exercise is to list all current and recent human resources efforts in the organization. Have senior management stand back and assess which of those efforts were driven by management as a key to implementing business strategy. How clear is the logical connection between what we have been doing in HR and the needs of the business to win in the marketplace? Too many line leaders see too many HR efforts as a cost of doing business rather than as core to successful implementation of strategy.

You might also ask HR professionals to explain the subtleties of the business strategy: Why will our current strategy make us successful? How might the strategy change to make us more successful?

3. How much impact does HR have today on our business results?

I certainly acknowledge that measuring HR efforts is not a science. I wish that I were better able to demonstrate how to do that. But I do know that at a minimum, management will have an intuitive sense of which of these efforts seem directly related to successfully implementing business strategy. If management and HR professionals cannot clearly make the case why a given HR effort helped the business, they should seriously question why it was done and the value of that investment.

4. Does our organization have an HR Plan? Who "owns" the HR Plan? What is the role of management in planning for and doing strategic human resources work?

In my role as a consultant, I always anticipate what I will see when I meet with leaders and ask them for a copy of the HR Plan. With rare exception, the HR leader either proudly produces a copy of the plan for the HR department or has no plan at all. I have yet to see anyone offer the HR component of the business plan that outlines what management feels is needed in the human and organizational arena in order to succeed in the marketplace. I have yet to look over a plan that is owned by line management, rather than by HR.

Of course, the HR department should also have a clear plan for its efforts. That, however, is not the HR Plan. That is the HR Department Plan. The HR Plan is a section of the organization's business plan. It should be owned by the head of the business and outline what needs to be done from a human resources perspective to support the business. The HR Department Plan outlines what the department will deliver in support of the overall business and HR Plan. There is a huge difference between the HR Plan for the organization and the HR Department Plan, although the HR Department Plan should be directly aligned to support the company's HR Plan. I discuss these differences in greater detail in Chapter 7.

5. *When line management needs help on people/organizational issues, to whom does it turn?*

To some, it seems obvious that line management would turn to its HR leaders to provide help on human resources issues. I am amazed at how often, in fact, managers turn elsewhere. Think, for example, about who provided the primary leadership for much of the work through the 1980s and 1990s on teams in the workplace. By and large, the impetus came from the department responsible for quality improvement. There were some HR groups that led this effort in their companies and some HR groups that got quickly on board, but the majority of this work was led by the quality function. And yet this was arguably one of the most strategic human efforts being done in industry during those years.

Who provides much of the leadership on the efforts to downsize many organizations? Once again, most efforts have been led by finance, not HR. Some might argue that such downsizing produced unsurprising results given that human dynamics and work design are not part of most finance professionals' expertise. Many organizations ended up hiring back far too many of the people they had let go.

6. *What is the current versus the right balance between HR advocacy of the employee and its advocacy of organizational purposes?*

This is one of HR's most difficult balancing acts—advocating for the employee and, at the same time, advocating for the organization. Some HR groups have clearly gone to the extreme of seeing HR's role as primarily an advocate for the employee. They play a paternalistic role, protecting employees from management. It almost becomes a pseudounion role. On the other hand, some HR groups have become so focused on the success of the business that they have forgotten the employee. Unfortunately, in far too many instances, this has become a polarizing issue.

HR must learn to balance the two; both are critical. They are intrinsically related to each other. The organization cannot succeed without the wholehearted energies and commitment of employees. The organization, at its core, is really a collection of employees: some managers and some individual contributors. Both are needed, and both are important.

On the other hand, the employees need the organization to be successful. Most organizations are not philanthropic by nature. In the long term, they must be financially viable if they are to maintain jobs for employees. And, beyond basic job security, most people simply want to be part of something that is successful. A manager once suggested that one of the best employee relations strategies that exists is a successful business. People love knowing that they are contributing to a winner. Unfortunately, HR too frequently falls into the trap of feeling that it needs to take one side or the other in this dilemma.

7. *What is the "political readiness" in our organization to transition HR to a more strategic role?*

This is crucial. HR transitions are difficult under the most favorable of conditions. If there are significant and powerful leaders within the organization who want to control or want to keep HR focused on administration, the change will be very difficult. If key leaders within HR itself are detractors from the change effort, these are important obstacles to identify early. In Chapter 17, I discuss these issues in greater detail.

8. *Who would be the sponsors for change, and why?*

The approach to changing an HR organization is quite different if the key sponsor for the change is a line manager, rather than someone within HR. If the change is coming not from the top of line management but from within senior or midmanagement, you need to think carefully about how to gain executive support. Obviously, if HR leadership has determined a need for change but does not yet have pull from the line, the process of engaging management must be carefully considered.

When a CEO has determined that this change is key for her business strategy, the change process tends to be drastically faster and more simplified. But I have seen several organizations where a CEO may ask for a change in the company's approach to HR and/or in the HR organization itself but frankly not have any idea what he has requested. When the hard questions come up, such leaders often shy away and do not offer the support that is needed. So engaging top leaders is about education as well as influence.

9. *How can we leverage the sponsors?*

Once sponsors are clearly identified, you want to develop a plan for how you will leverage their influence in a successful transition. Obviously, a CEO has a tremendous amount of power in the organization, but every CEO approaches the work differently depending upon his own management style and the culture of the organization. Whoever the sponsor is, you need to be clear about what has proven most successful in the past as that person has sponsored particular efforts and what hasn't worked so well for her. Particularly if the sponsor is not the CEO, you want to be thoughtful about how the sponsor tends to influence best, what help she needs, and how you can supply that help.

10. *Who would be the detractors, and why?*

On the one hand, it seems hard for many of us HR enthusiasts to believe that there would be detractors to any effort that is designed to improve the performance of the organization. But they are there. They exist in the line management, within the employee base, and within the HR organization itself.

Why would a line manager become a detractor? There are a variety of reasons. I believe that, first and foremost, we need to realize that over the recent decades of automating (and therefore making public) much of the line managers' data, much of the HR arena represents the last function for which they can hold their cards close to the vest. There are aspects of strategic human resources that they perceive will put new pressures on them as they manage their organization. These include:

- How they manage their budget and head count

- Visibility of and pressure on their own management style

- Their ability to maintain control of their organization

- The potential for structural (and therefore career) changes

- The need to fund new projects for which they don't understand the ROI

All of these issues and more have the potential to make the line manager nervous about a change to strategic HR. Again, I discuss managing the political whirlpools of HR change efforts in greater detail in Chapter 17.

Sometimes employees misinterpret a change to strategic human resources as "HR has now become a tool of management and cannot represent us any longer." Or they may decide, "This proves that management cares only about making money and doesn't care about the employee." These feelings come up particularly in organizations where HR has played a paternalistic role.

Finally, HR professionals can feel troubled about the change effort because they see it as a threat to an otherwise safe and stable career path. Many don't understand the changes and are fearful that they will be negatively impacted. Some feel their work or role will decrease in value. Some just disagree that this is the right direction to take HR.

11. *How can we work with the detractors?*

As you identify individuals who might be potential detractors, you want to develop a specific plan on how to deal with the issues or concerns that they have. This may include taking time to coach and help them understand the changes and how they will benefit from them. It may include having other peers of the concerned persons discuss and resolve their issues with them. It may include using senior leadership more to make it clear that these changes are part of the new strategy and must be implemented. Most likely, you will come up with specific solutions to the specific issues that they have. The important thing is not to ignore the fact that there will be detractors and that you can improve the situation by coming up with a plan to deal with their concerns.

All of these questions need to be answered honestly—brutally honestly—to make your assessment useful and to develop a plan to successfully implement your changes.

Organizational Readiness Survey

In addition to considering the previous eleven questions, you may find the following survey about the current state of organizational readiness for change useful in helping you gain insight into others' opinions. Getting input from a subset of HR professionals, employees, and managers might prove useful. Once again, responses must be brutally honest.

	1 = Strongly Disagree 5 = Strongly Agree				
My organization says that people are critical to its success.	1	2	3	4	5
My organization behaves as though people are critical to its success.	1	2	3	4	5
My company has a clear HR Plan that is linked to business strategy.	1	2	3	4	5

(continues)

The senior-level line leaders feel ownership of the HR Plan.	1	2	3	4	5
Management is engaged in the development of human resources strategies.	1	2	3	4	5
Our HR organization contributes positively to key business initiatives.	1	2	3	4	5
Our HR organization is proactive in leading needed change.	1	2	3	4	5
Our company shares a common human resources theory base and language.	1	2	3	4	5
Our HR organization's work is well aligned with the business.	1	2	3	4	5
Our HR organization strikes an appropriate balance between employee and business advocacy.	1	2	3	4	5
Our HR organization coordinates all of its various efforts and programs well.	1	2	3	4	5
Our HR organization is clearly moving to a strategic role.	1	2	3	4	5
Our company has the right HR talent to be truly strategic.	1	2	3	4	5

Sharing the Analysis

Analysis of these two sets of questions won't capture everything necessary to understand the context and history of a particular organization. But it will produce a stronger initial perspective on the strengths and weaknesses of an HR group and management readiness to partner with HR professionals. Wherever possible, the honest assessment that comes from these questions should be openly discussed between the head of HR and the senior-most line manager.

Ideally, they will share a common view on how to approach the change. In some cases, the line leader will have done this type of analysis and may believe that he cannot make the needed changes with the HR talent that exists in the organization today. In some cases, the change strategy will begin with the need to change HR leadership. Where this is the case, the leadership change should happen first, and then the CEO and new HR leader can plan together the change effort.

I recall one organization where top management decided that it wanted a new approach to human resources. It said that it wanted to do whatever it took to make such a change. It even took the very difficult step of removing an ineffective HR leader from the role. However, it bowed to political pressure when it came to that person's replacement and chose someone who had significant political support, despite the fact that the candidate personally admitted to having neither the inclination nor the skills to lead a strategic HR change. Too many HR change efforts fail because of concessions to political pressure about HR leadership.

In some cases, it is the HR leader who sees the need for change, but the senior-most line leader is the major obstacle to the change. Obviously, the HR person is not likely to replace the CEO. (When that is done, it is generally with the help of the board and generally for reasons far broader than the CEO's lack of insight into strategic human resources.) I have known HR leaders who have very patiently worked with line leaders to help them see the significant impact upon future business results. Sometimes this has proven successful and well worth the time.

I have also seen some HR leaders work for years to change the views of a line leader who just doesn't seem to understand strategic human resources. Some HR leaders finally choose to abandon their vision and acknowledge that they will not likely accomplish with this CEO all that they would like to do. However, they believe that the organization is better off with at least one strategic HR voice than with none at all. Others get to a point where they simply acknowledge that this CEO wants something different from what they want, and the HR leader makes a personal choice to change employment and find a partner who really is ready for what he has to offer. These are some of the most difficult decisions that an HR leader will ever make. These are often choices where the HR leader and all around them come to understand the depth of their commitment to the changing human resources field.

I am asked on occasion if there is anything that I might discover during an assessment of organizational readiness that would influence me to decide not to move forward with a change effort. There is one potential outcome of the assessment that would most likely cause me to stop and not move forward until it had been resolved. That is the need for support and advocacy from senior line management. That is a must. If line management doesn't want a more strategic HR focus, I just don't believe you can get there. As I mentioned, some HR people are more patient than others. Some will spend their career working to get line management to the right place. I would be willing to give that goal some time, but at some point I would want to be smart enough to recognize that this old dog just doesn't want to learn new tricks— feels no need to learn new tricks—and therefore most likely never will. If that is the case, I'd move on to a different organization where I could have an impact.

In summary, the CEO and an HR leader can never hope to transform an HR organization without understanding where the organization is today and how it got there. Then they can position the change effort with the appropriate focus, pace, and intensity to fit that particular organization.

CHAPTER FOUR

Develop a Framework and Language for HR

J. STUART BLACK AND HAL B. GREGERSEN have written, "Unlocking individual change starts and ends with the mental maps people carry in their heads—how they see the organization and their jobs. Just as actual maps guide the steps people take on a hike through the Himalayas, mental maps direct people's behavior in daily organizational life. And if leaders cannot change individuals' mental maps, they will not change the destinations people pursue or the paths they take to get there."[1]

This component of transforming an HR organization deals heavily with mental maps—making them explicit and offering a common one. While my primary focus in this book is on practical application, I am quick to acknowledge the need for any change to be built upon good theory and sound conceptual frameworks. Great execution based upon inadequate theory, strategy, or frameworks will not ultimately be useful. Climbing a ladder to the top of the building only to find that the ladder is leaning against the wrong building is not a very successful climb.

My experience is that truly effective strategic HR leaders are very capable in their understanding and creation of theories and models. Sometimes they may borrow from others' work, and sometimes they may create their own. Whatever the case, they are able to take the complexity of organizational life and use principles and frameworks to simplify it, creating a common language within the organization.

A Framework Helps Everyone Speak the Same Language

Although they usually aren't conscious of it, line managers, HR professionals, and other employees naturally test what HR does against a standard in their own heads that is probably based upon some personally held principles or frameworks. Expectations are difficult to fulfill while they remain hidden. And communication can be frustrated by a lack of shared terms. By introducing a common language and framework, HR leaders make expectations explicit and enable the HR group to work more effectively. It is particularly helpful to use a visual model so that people from widely different backgrounds can conceptualize these ideas in the same way. This has been one of the key elements lacking in human resources to date.

Above all, this language and model must be practical and easy to understand. Without exception, my experience is that neither line management nor employees want a lot of theory. They want things to make sense. An HR professional with a superb mind will still be tossed out if he can't bring it down to earth.

Creating Your Own HR Framework

Perhaps an initial question that a serious HR professional should ask herself is how much time she spends acquiring the good thoughts of others. This is not to say that our own principles and frameworks should be mirror reflections of others' thoughts. I believe that the best frameworks are built by an individual who has benefited from the thoughts of many other people, yet who has developed a framework that works well for her. Sometimes her own experience will lead her to reject commonly accepted theory and come up with something different that actually works better in practice.

A starting point for serious strategic HR practitioners is the body of existing theories and principles, which can be used to create one's own personalized principles and frameworks. (In the Appendix, I recommend articles and books for foundational theory in strategic human resources.) I have leaned heavily on the thinking of great leaders, academics, and consultants in developing my own principles, frameworks, and applications. My attempts in this area produced a set of baseline philosophies or principles that have driven my work over much of the past two decades.

Like many of us who read a great deal and then debate, apply, test, rethink, and reapply, I often find it difficult to recall specifically which ideas came from which sources. In this book, I make every effort to acknowledge contributions where I can. The most useful theories, principles, and applications are the culmination of countless bits of input that come together in strange and often unexpected ways as needs arise.

The Fundamental Roots of a Human Resources Theory Base

I have greatly appreciated the insight of C. K. Prahalad at a lecture I heard many years ago where he raised the question "What is the fundamental theory base of human resources?" Prahalad's position was that until HR becomes clear on this question, it will continue to wander in the wilderness, making attempts to influence, but without much success. He noted that, at that time, many leaders in other business functions were much clearer about the theory base that drove their field than HR leaders were.

Finance, for example, has the basic theory base of "investment with the expectation of return," or something similar to that. This may or may not be as much explicitly taught as it is intuitively understood. Nonetheless, most finance professionals start with this common understanding. Around this very simple theory base, the finance discipline is able to design processes and methodologies to plan for capital, to budget within the organization, to track and account for the actual spending against budget, to measure, and so on. HR traditionally has not had such a clear, simple theory base upon which to design its processes, methodologies, and tools.

So what is the fundamental theory base for human resources? Prahalad suggested that some HR leaders would describe the human resources theory base as basically that of individual psychology, focused entirely upon individual motivation and individual fulfillment. Another group would argue that sociology is the human resources theory base, focusing on the dynamics of small groups of people working together in small organizational communities. Another group of people would consider human resources to be fundamentally founded around a theory base of employee advocacy—hearing the voice of the people and protecting them from the evils of management and the organization. Yet another group would focus primarily on company advocacy, believing that the principal work of HR professionals is to focus on organizational or company effectiveness. Still others would define HR's role as essentially administrative, with no reason to be involved in the key aspects of business strategy at all.

Most of us have observed and/or lived in HR organizations that obviously follow for the most part one of these theory bases. Generally, HR groups don't tend to be terribly explicit about which theory base they have accepted, usually because they aren't conscious that they have made a choice. However, it doesn't take much observation to clearly see what it is. There is a vast difference in the emphasis and behavior of an HR group that fundamentally believes, for example, that HR is about protecting the employee compared to those of an HR group that is focused primarily on developing the employee or on building effective teams. It shows in everything that the department does.

In summary, HR has struggled to develop a coherent set of principles or theory base. Is it:

- Psychology?
- Sociology?
- Legal theory?
- Employee advocacy?
- Company advocacy?

While aspects of each of these theory bases rightfully influences the field, they lack the integrated focus that makes them as powerful as they might be.

A Set of Principles for Strategic Human Resources

I have found the following five principles useful in directing my efforts in strategic human resources. (I have borrowed heavily from Prahalad's presentation in the first principles.)

1. Talent is the engine behind the creation of all value.
2. Every business issue (problem and opportunity) is a symptom of deeper human or organizational issues.
3. Talent will be the resource of scarcity in the future.
4. All human resources work must be directly connected to the business strategy and customer needs.
5. Line management is responsible for human resources work in the organization.

Let us look at each of these points more closely.

1. *Talent is the engine behind the creation of all value.* Understanding and accepting this principle is fundamental to moving toward strategic human resources. The creation of anything of value comes about through human talent. Products and services are conceived,

designed, manufactured, and sold by people. Ultimately, nothing is done that isn't initiated by people. If that is true, it is clear that the effective management of people and the talent base that they represent is at the source of creating value.

I am always amazed at how some leaders seem to separate the "business issues" from the "people issues." They have lost sight of the reality that there is no business issue or opportunity without people. There is no business without people. They are one and the same. Viewed this way, anything and everything that HR professionals do should be focused on developing and leveraging human competence or talent to create value by whatever definition the organization might pose.

Application of this theory base demands that HR leadership be capable of adding value in any and all organizational circumstances. It is not enough to be present at the table just as the "expert on people issues," to sit and wait until a "people problem" comes up, and then get engaged in the discussion. HR leadership today needs to be capable of adding value in all areas—contributing to product development, to market strategy, to financial analysis, and so on. While leveraging human talent will remain the HR practitioners' primary domain expertise, HR leadership will never succeed at the strategic level until it develops some expertise in all other aspects of business, as well. It is impossible to appropriately design processes outside the context of the organizational need. This principle is an open invitation for the HR leader to become involved in and add value to all aspects of the business.

2. *Every business issue (problem and opportunity) is a symptom of deeper human or organizational issues.* Behind this principle is an assumption that most business leaders spend much of their time dealing with a wide range of important business symptoms. The symptoms can vary. It might be that sales are off. It might be that profitability is down. Perhaps product quality is down. Or the

company has lost touch with the customer. Whatever the symptom is, there is a human or organizational solution at its core.

- If sales are off, we may want to ask what is it about our people who are doing market research, developing product, or selling product that is not meeting the needs of customers, who ultimately make the decision to buy or not.

- When product quality is down, that's a very serious symptom, perhaps of an organizational process that is not right, or an indication that skills of people need to be developed.

- If we are losing market share, we should ask whether we have the executive talent needed to understand the customer and the competition.

Every example of what we generally call a business problem is ultimately a human resources issue.

In my consulting work, I often provide the front page of the *Wall Street Journal* to HR leaders. I invite them to pick any article on the page. We then work together to see how the particular issue discussed in the article might be viewed as a symptom with a clear human and/or organizational root solution. I have yet to see the article or issue that does not fit this pattern. A good HR leader has developed the innate ability to see the human resources implications in every business issue. HR leaders who have not built this skill will continue to sit on the sidelines with little influence.

3. *Talent will be the resource of scarcity in the future.* Finding talent over the course of the next two decades will be one of the greatest challenges that organizational leaders will face. These leaders will find it far easier to find capital and technical resources than talent. I am not talking about finding someone to simply fill the space. By talent, I mean people who clearly bring the right competencies (skills, knowledge, and aptitudes) that are vitally needed to fulfill the business strategy. Companies will also need to attract and retain the group of employees who do a good solid job—those who are not the superstars but who make the organization function.

CEOs desperately need human resources leaders who can ensure that the processes are in place to attract and retain talent over the long haul. This talent management must be integrally connected to the business strategy if the strategy is to be successfully implemented.

4. *All human resources work must be directly connected to the business strategy and customer needs.* In large, complex organizations, all human resources work must be done in the context of how it will help leverage human competence to meet organizational, and therefore, customer objectives. Too often, HR can become internally focused and eager to try out the latest human resources technology or program. Sometimes, those efforts, on closer examination, do not necessarily align with customer needs and the key purposes of the larger organization.

This certainly is not to say that HR can focus on organizational needs at the neglect of the individual employee. In fact, it is clear to most leaders that they will never meet their business goals without satisfied and motivated employees. HR leaders must learn to integrate the needs of the individual and those of the organization. They must be careful not to polarize the role of HR as being focused exclusively on the employee or on the organization. It must balance the two interests.

5. *Line management is responsible for human resources work in the organization.* The fifth principle asserts that human resources leadership really begins at the top of the organization. The HR functional leader should never be viewed as the person who ultimately is responsible for all the people work in the organization. The CEO or the head of the organization is the senior human resources leader of the organization and must be viewed that way. No CEO should look at her HR leader as though this is the person who will handle all of the people issues so that she doesn't have to worry about them. That would be just as absurd as saying the CEO doesn't care at all about the financial issues because the

CFO will sort through all of them. Rather, both the CFO and the head of HR will do everything that needs to be done in terms of strategy, systems, measurements, and planning to ensure that the finances and the people aspects of the organization are well planned and well managed. But the CEO is ultimately responsible.

Some line and HR leaders have taken this concept to an extreme by assuming that there is no need for an HR department at all, since management will do this work. In most cases, this strategy cannot succeed. It is highly unlikely that a line leader of an organization has enough technical insight into the people issues of the organization to deal with them without any help from a "technical expert." This is no different from a line leader's need to have someone provide technical leadership in product development, finance, or marketing. While the rhetoric exists in many organizations that people work is line management work, the practice is too often missing.

My Strategic Human Resources Framework

Over the years, I have found that, even with the existing variety of models that describe human resources work and roles, I still needed one that would connect the work of the business with the work of the HR professional. I therefore have worked to develop my own framework that provides a simple yet useful way for line and HR leaders to talk about and understand strategic human resources. I wanted it to illustrate a clear relationship among human resources work, the business strategy, and the business environment, which includes the customer. I also needed to identify specific HR processes that could impact strategy fulfillment.

This model is presented in Figure 4-1. To begin at the top, every business organization exists in some business environment. This environment includes consumers, customers, retail outlets, competitors, government regulations, and a variety of other conditions in which we

Figure 4-1. Strategic human resources framework.

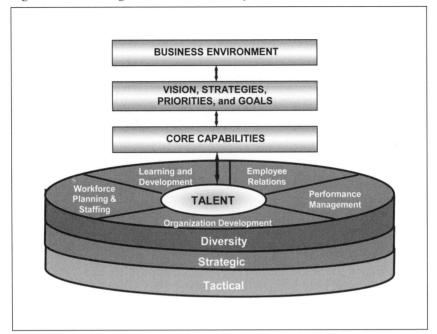

all do business. The effective HR professional is intimately familiar with the environment, especially the customer. He understands that everything that he does in his human resources work must ultimately promote meeting the needs of the customer better than the competition.

In the context of that business environment, every organization needs to develop its own business strategy, priorities, and goals that allow it to win in that environment. The effectiveness of the strategy is ultimately measured by its ability to lead customers to buy that organization's goods or services, rather than the competition's. Everything that HR employees or any employees do in organizations must be linked to successfully implementing the business strategy.

For an organization to implement its strategies, it must have a set of core capabilities that support those strategies. By capabilities, I am not referring to the competencies or skills and knowledge of individual employees. I am referring to fundamental core abilities that the organization has developed as an entity. The uniqueness and strength of these abilities determine an organization's capacity to differentiate, compete, and win in the marketplace.

One example of such a capability is the ability of a given organization to move new products to market very quickly. Another might be the capacity to manufacture in unique and creative ways. A third example is the capability to distribute a tremendous number of product sets across a very complex set of retail outlets. A firm in the financial services industry might, for example, need to greatly increase its points of distribution in order to stay competitive. For a company such as Hallmark, which moves a tremendous number of products to a large number of outlets, the capability to distribute lots of products to lots of rooftops is critical in order for the company to stay competitive.

Organizational capabilities are created through a coordination of the people, technological, and financial resources of a company. Hence, we have the link between winning in the marketplace and talent. The central work of leadership is to effectively manage people in order to develop corporate capabilities that allow them to win in the marketplace. Everything that the HR organization does should be focused on leveraging those human competencies to create capabilities that allow the organization to win with its strategy in the marketplace. This is what is known as the vertical alignment between talent and the marketplace. This particular framework emphasizes the need for HR leadership to ensure that any human resources work, whether done by the HR group or by line management, is focused on leveraging human talent to win in the marketplace.

The Five Fundamental Human Resources Processes

The model in Figure 4-1 depicts the circle that is called the horizontal dimension of the human resources framework. I have found it useful to divide human resources work into five fundamental processes. (There are other useful ways to map out and label human resources work. I am less concerned about these being the precise five than I am about people finding a framework that works for them.) The five human resources processes that I have used are:

1. *Workforce Planning and Staffing.*

   The process of fulfilling current talent needs and projecting/planning for future talent needs given the business strategy is critical. It includes developing methods to attract, integrate, and retain that talent.

2. *Learning and Development.*

   Ensuring that the company has the specific talent it needs at the time it needs it is an important process. Talent needs change over time. Some have said that the shelf life for most professional skills is no more than three to five years. There is a critical need for a learning and development process to continue building existing talent.

3. *Organization Development.*

   This process examines organizational processes and systems to ensure that they are aligned with business strategy. Planning, measurement, structure, work flows, and budgets can all be developed to enable talent more effectively.

4. *Performance Management.*

   Once the essential talent and processes are established in the organization, an effective process for managing performance is needed to ensure that the organization gets the outcomes that it desires.

5. *Employee Relations.*

   This process focuses on the needs of individual employees, providing support so that employees can work effectively and sustain their efforts over time. It is also about managing the relationship between the employee and the needs of the larger organization.

With these five processes, I am referring to human resources processes and not to the HR organization. Whether an organization has an HR group or not, I would still use these same five processes. In other words, no matter who does the work, this is the work that needs to be done. These five processes are dealt with in detail in Chapters 9–13.

About Diversity

There is a complex debate regarding diversity and how it fits into an overall strategic human resources model. There are some who would suggest that diversity is the sixth process. I discuss this perspective in Chapter 17. Advocates of this position tend to want to see diversity listed as another human resources function alongside workforce planning and staffing, performance management, employee relations, learning and development, and organization development. Others believe diversity is more of a mind-set, an important outcome, or a way of approaching human issues, rather than an actual work process.

At Hallmark, we concluded that, while diversity is a critical aspect of human resources work, it is not a process in the same sense as the other five areas. In fact, we concluded that it is an integral component of each of the five processes and hence designed it into this framework as supporting and cutting across all five.

For example, it is impossible to develop an effective workforce or staffing plan without taking into account the critical aspects of diversity. Does a specific staffing plan strengthen or weaken the company position from a diversity perspective? Much of diversity work is done through education—learning and development—to build awareness and new skills. Diversity has obvious implications in the arena of employee relations. An employee who feels that she has been discriminated against will not be as effective in work as one who feels that there are no artificial barriers to accomplishing her job. Similar examples could be given for organization development and performance management. At Hallmark, we concluded that diversity was an important enough issue that it should be included in the thinking of every human resources process and not viewed as a separate, stand-alone effort.

Managing and Integrating These Five Levers

These five processes are the levers that each organization has at its disposal to maximize its talent and the competencies that individuals bring to win in the marketplace. The management of these levers is critical. It should receive at least the same level of management attention as any other aspect of the business, such as product development, technology, or marketing.

It is also vital to pay careful attention to how these five human resource processes interact. They must be viewed as an integrated system, rather than as five distinct and individual processes. Whenever an HR leader develops a proposal in one of these five process areas, it is essential that the proposal explain the implications for the other four human resources processes. For example, an organization development effort that would redesign some aspect of the work flow or organization must include in the analysis the impact of the proposal on the other four processes. This includes analysis of the implications for attracting, integrating, retaining, and developing needed talent, the impact on existing employees' well-being, and the ability to manage performance in the new organizational process. It is impossible to implement a program involving any one of these processes without its having implications for the others.

While at Hallmark, I worked hard to push my HR leaders to bring only proposals that clarified the implications of their arena of work for each of the other arenas. I didn't want to support a pattern in which HR designed programs and processes that were disconnected from the other HR processes.

Strategic and Tactical Aspects of Human Resources Work

The final aspect of this model is an acknowledgment that every one of these five processes has both a strategic and a tactical component. Too many people hold the view that organization development and perhaps learning and development represent the strategic components of the people equation, while other areas, such as benefits, represent the tactical components. I have long since come to understand how wrong that assumption is.

Using benefits as an example, though I am far from an expert, I have come to understand the incredibly strategic aspect of benefits. In many companies, there are millions or even billions of dollars' worth of assets tied up in the benefits programs. At a minimum, then, this area is strategic just because of the raw costs involved. But, perhaps even more important, we should step back and ask ourselves what potential motivational impact that hundreds of millions of benefits dollars might have on people. As we examined the motivational impact of our benefits program at Hallmark, it became evident that the design of the benefits programs said much about the strategic assumptions that leaders make about employees and their relationship to the business entity.

Every aspect of human resources work has a strategic component, and every aspect of human resources work has a tactical component. It is essential that work in each of these arenas be integrated at both the strategic and the tactical levels. As long as HR divisions continue to think of themselves as being either strategic or tactical, they will not progress.

Using this framework gave HR professionals at Hallmark a clearer understanding of the connection between human resources work and business strategy. It provided an invaluable language, giving HR professionals and line leaders in our organization a way to talk about different needs and different roles. It allowed line managers and HR professionals to start from essentially the same place in our efforts to change HR. Without this common starting point, we would not have been able to make the changes that were ultimately made.

Developing a Framework that's Useful for You

Again, I do not believe that the human resources framework I have proposed is the only one that can work. I do not propose it as a framework that every HR group should necessarily adopt. I deeply believe that you need to struggle through the development of your own framework so that you know it inside and out. And you need a process by which you will know how to respond to all of the hard questions that undoubtedly will be asked. It has to be intuitive for you. You cannot simply copy someone else's. That just doesn't work.

Whatever your framework is, it needs to respond to the following questions:

- How does HR work connect with the business strategy?
- What are the components of HR work?
- How do those components work together?

As long as these needs are addressed, the only other important thing is that you find a way that works for you to talk about human resources work within HR and with line managers and employees.

In summary, here is a checklist to help you develop and clarify your own human resources model:

- Does your organization have a clear framework for strategic human resources?
- If so, is it widely used and recognized?
- Is it reinforced in everything that HR does?
- Does it provide a high-level understanding of the role of human resources work and the HR group, without getting into too many of the tactics in the organization?

In the process of addressing these questions, you can create a common starting point that will enable your HR transformation to get up and running much more quickly.

Note

1. J. Stuart Black and Hal B. Gregersen, *Leading Strategic Change: Breaking Through the Brain Barrier* (London: Financial Times/Prentice Hall, 2003), p. 7.

CHAPTER FIVE

Understand the Senior HR Leader's Role as Organizational Architect

WHETHER TACIT OR EXPLICIT, certain questions surface on a regular basis for those who fill the top HR job in an organization:

- How do I ensure that I am successful in this role?

- Do I keep doing what has made me successful in the past?

- Surely there must be something that I do in this job that is significantly different from what I have been doing in the past. What is it?

- How do I develop the influence skills that will be needed to make a real difference to the business?

Answers to these questions are generally hard to come by. Those working within an HR organization may ask other questions:

- What should the leader of this HR organization be doing to position our group more strategically?

- How do I manage a boss who is not yet thinking about HR strategically?

The top HR leader in an organization is uniquely positioned to set the stage for strategic business partnership. In many ways, the strategic influence of an HR organization depends heavily on the strategic influence of that top HR leader.

The senior HR generalist in an organization, or the head of HR, is often named the vice president of HR (VP-HR) or chief people officer. The VP-HR sets the stage for what is done throughout the rest of the HR organization. The degree to which this leader spends his time on tactics influences the HR organization's ability to think and work strategically. When the senior leader is deeply involved in developing business strategy and leveraging strategic human resources work throughout the business, those in the HR organization can be far more strategic themselves and with greater impact.

Access Needed by the VP-HR

In general, for the leader of HR to play a truly strategic role, she should report to the CEO. In some organizations, the head of HR reports to an administrative leader. The rationale may be the need to manage a reasonable span of control. However, it is an assessment of the value, or lack of value, that HR is perceived to bring. As with any other VP (e.g., finance, operations, marketing), the VP-HR should sit as a member of the business team and contribute to the overall direction and operations of the business.

My concern on this point is actually less about structure than it is about access. However an organization is structured, the head of HR must have access and must be able to contribute, as the other functional and business heads do, to the development and implementation of the business strategy. Why does the head of HR need access to the business conversation? Simple. It is impossible to translate a business strategy into people and organizational strategies and programs if one is not intimately aware of the subtleties of the business conversation and debate. It simply cannot be done. Conversely, it is a rare head of administration or finance who can sit at the business table in an HR leader's stead and appropriately translate strategy into human resources terms.

Organizational structure that separates the HR leader from the business conversation tends to produce a very tactical HR organization over time. It is challenging enough for an effective HR leader to be strategic when she knows the specifics of the business. When HR leaders have to pick up pieces secondhand and only piecemeal at that, they simply cannot make the needed strategic connections.

In my experience, unless the HR leader has access to the business table, any desires to play the role of organizational architect will be futile. For those who find themselves in this position, my best advice is to start by gaining access to the table. As I mentioned earlier, this is best done by demonstrating the level of skill and insight that makes it clear to others that you truly add value to the business conversation.

To be successful, the VP-HR needs to understand the marketplace, product offerings, technology, and investment strategy to the same degree as all other executives at the table. In addition to understanding the strategic issues of the business, the VP-HR should have a well-honed point of view about the future direction of the organization. Her voice should be one that adds value to the conversations and debates over business strategy and tactics. Certainly, the VP-HR has his own specialty in the arena of human and organizational issues. But this is no different from the marketing and finance VPs' having their specialties in the arenas of marketing and finance. They still need to understand the business environment and the strategic choices the organization is making.

In addition to her involvement in the development of business strategy, the VP-HR should lead the process to interpret the business strategy into a robust human resources strategy for the company. Again, this is true for other generalists, as well—the VP-Finance should ensure that overall business strategy becomes interpreted into financial strategy for the company, for example.

The VP-HR wants to be careful, however, not to be the only or even primary creator of the HR plan and therefore the only one who feels responsibility for its fulfillment. There are far too many HR plans that are created by HR leaders and not really understood, let alone owned, by line management. Ideally, she will extensively involve key senior leadership, as described in Chapter 7.

What Does an Organizational Architect Do?

Perhaps the greatest differentiator between other functional leaders and the VP-HR is the role that the VP-HR plays as an "organizational architect." What does an organizational architect do? She sets the conceptual and political stage for accomplishing any work related to organizational issues or talent. She sees her role at a higher level than the technologist who simply carries out a human resources project. The VP-HR needs to look at the overall functioning of the organization, observe organizational needs, and provide the leadership needed to address those needs—even when they fall outside the traditional purview of human resources work.

One of the distinguishing abilities of the VP-HR who acts as an organizational architect is the capability to work at and across organizational, conceptual, and cultural boundaries. She is able to see the interconnectedness of various discrete elements. In so doing, she looks well beyond the "people stuff" and looks at the entire system. She must also be conversant with the workings of the entire organization so as to be able to provide solutions to these "non–HR" issues. Someone may ask at this point, "Why in the world does HR care about issues beyond 'the people stuff'?" An organizational architect has, by definition, chosen to think about issues that cut across the entire spectrum of the organization. Some may argue that all leaders should view themselves as "organizational architects." Though that's a valid point, I believe that the VP-HR, alongside other executives, plays a particular role that is different from that of all other functional leaders. The VP-HR should bring specific technical skills in the arena of people and organizations. He should lead out in this architectural role.

Organizational Architecture Is About Alignment

Perhaps the greatest contribution of the organizational architect is the ability to see and then help manage the alignment of customer needs; business strategy; and organizational objectives, processes, systems, and structures. This work of alignment is what differentiates the architect from the technician. The architect sees and is able to influence the relationship between each of the critical systems and processes. Hence the need to be an effective systemic thinker. The role of organizational architect is less of a formal role than it is a mind-set, a combination of abilities.

What might be some examples of an HR architect doing work outside the classic people arena and identifying needs across the entire system? Let me highlight a couple of examples at a very high level.

An Example: Strengthening Marketing Capabilities

At Hallmark, many leaders recognized the need to rethink the company's approach to marketing and brand management. We needed better marketing capabilities and a stronger connection with the customer and the marketplace. When I discussed this issue with my OD director, it was clear to us that one aspect of the problem was some structural or design elements that would need to change in order to develop better marketing capabilities.

Strong and visible leadership was needed to ensure that the right people came together to address this issue. My role as organizational architect meant that I needed to:

- See the need and legitimize addressing it.

- Align with other business leaders to identify specific needs.

- Frame up the issues and potential solutions.

- Align resources (inside and outside) to make the needed changes.

- Help in project management.

- Coach leaders.

In some organizations, HR might easily label such issues as "marketing's problem." But I did not view this as a "marketing issue." This was an issue about organizational capabilities, about organizational effectiveness. It impacted the entire system.

So I worked with the head of marketing and with the president to form a coalition of support for the change effort. The head of marketing was clear about the need for a change to our marketing approach. He was less clear about how to get it focused. This became the role of HR—to provide a process to align support for change.

Although HR remained involved in a support role and even as part of the oversight group, the responsibility for the effort clearly belonged to the president and to the VP-Marketing. They ultimately made and owned the decisions. For the VP-HR, the shift from a strong initial leadership role to a more subtle influence role was critical to ensure that ownership remains with line management.

Another Example: Reexamining Our Business Model

Another example at Hallmark was HR's recognition of the need to reexamine the basic business model of the corporation. It was clear that our current business model was not working across all of the various businesses and that this shortcoming needed to be addressed. HR identified the need and provided management with a conceptual framework to understand the need for the change. Management made it clear that it wanted to lead the effort for a changed business model. HR once again identified resources that could be brought in to support this effort. HR facilitated the process to review and select a consultant. But, again, management owned it now. I describe this effort in more detail in Chapter 11.

Organizational Architect Frames the Issue but Does Not Own It

These two examples raise one of the most challenging issues for the organizational architect: How far and how explicitly should you drive an issue?

The strategic HR leader sees broad organizational needs that other line leaders may not see. She needs to transfer this observation and the ownership to resolve it to the line owners as soon as possible. If she does not do this, the change effort will be viewed as an HR effort and will not likely ever accomplish what is needed. As long as HR maintains ownership, it is easy for line management to defer responsibility and the need to make hard decisions.

However, after ownership is transferred, line leaders may not make the decisions that the HR leader believes need to be made, due to politics or other influences. Leading change through influence, rather than direct control, certainly involves trade-offs. I don't see any way to get around it. In the end, I would rather push management to consciously address difficult decisions and set the stage for them to successfully make these decisions than miss the issue altogether and by default forgo the chance for change. Line leaders may not always make the decisions I would, but my role is to bring them to address the issue and make a decision.

Summary Points

- An organizational architect sees things that other business leaders don't, because she brings a systemic view to the work, looking across boundaries and pulling disparate parts together.

- The early phases of a change effort often require a strong leadership role from HR to identify the need and to garner the support and resources needed to get the work done.

- HR must ensure that the ultimate owners of significant organizational efforts are line leaders.

- After issues are transitioned to management ownership, it is difficult to predict the outcome, particularly with politically charged issues. You cannot know with absolute surety the outcome of the effort when ownership is transferred—yet it must be transferred.

A Different Power Base for the Organizational Architect

Many VPs-HR have come to their roles on the technical strength that they built in a specific HR area, for example, compensation, labor relations, or organization development. Most VPs-HR are tempted to continue using their technical strengths as their key power base as a VP. This is generally a great mistake. In so doing, they continue in their role as a supertechnician and never step up to the role of architect. They become known as a resource for a specific need and are not viewed as key leaders in the business.

Given that my personal technical strengths were in the area of organization development, there were times when I really wanted to play the lead OD role in some of the change efforts at Hallmark. (I discuss this in greater detail in Chapter 14.) I realized that I simply couldn't keep falling into my old OD role. I had a very competent OD director for the organization in Ellen Karp. I had to give her the space to do what she does so well. I had to build my power base upon my ability to set the stage for an OD effort, not upon being the OD consultant.

The power base for the VP-HR changes from technical expertise to the ability to see and frame up business issues for management in a way that leads to resolution. A VP-HR who continually relies on his technical prowess as a power base will become so engrossed in the details of specific projects that he will not be able to lead in other areas across the company.

Characteristics of an Effective VP-HR

There are a variety of characteristics that are critical in the top HR job. The following self-assessment questions may be helpful for the VP-HR who wants to determine whether she has them.

1. *Do I see the VP-HR role as an organizational architect?*

The VP-HR leader should consider it his responsibility to understand the full spectrum of business opportunities and issues and then identify their human and organizational implications. The great ones have an uncanny sixth sense and are able to interpret any business issue into its human and organizational implications. They are then able to set the political stage for the human resources work that is needed. They are able to help others see the connection that they see between the need and the answer. They are able to align resources to address the issue.

This does not mean that they have all of the answers. They generally don't. In fact, one of the greatest obstacles for many HR leaders is an assumption that they need to have the answers to the issues that they raise. They rarely do. This assumption keeps the HR leader from ever moving forward. The key to being an architect is understanding that you don't need to have all the detailed answers. You do need to see the issue and align resources for its resolution.

2. *Do I help develop business strategy?*

The VP-HR should be integrally involved in the development of the business strategy. An effective VP-HR intuitively understands process and therefore should be able to add unique skills around the process of developing strategy. In addition to helping with the process, she needs to contribute some content regarding the strategic direction of the enterprise. This is often more difficult. This requires the VP-HR leader to take extra time to become acquainted with all of the issues of the business. Obviously, this does not mean that she becomes the content expert for each area. However, she should be clear on a high-level framework of the business model and each organizational component's role in contributing to the model. HR leaders equipped with these insights are prepared to participate in a meaningful way to the development of strategy.

3. Do I understand well the organization's marketplace?

Every business leader should understand the dynamics of the marketplace. The VP-HR is no different. The VP-HR needs to understand the thought behind the market segmentation that is likely being led out of the marketing organization. If the VP-HR does not have a clear conception of the end customer for the business, he cannot contribute meaningfully to strategy development or organization design recommendations. The assumptions behind customer segmentation and customer needs offer critical clues into the desired organization design.

In addition to the organization design implications, the marketplace also gives great insights into the type of talent that an organization will need in the future. Many businesses have failed because they failed to see the changes in the customers' needs and desires and never had talent on board that could respond to those changes.

How can the VP-HR stay in touch with the marketplace? Quite simply, he stays in touch by staying in touch. He has to regularly spend time in the marketplace. He gets to know the customers, distributors, and vendors. He spends lots of time at retail if that is part of his organization's distribution. He simply has to find ways to be involved in the marketplace in which his business is involved.

4. *Do I have a working/conversant insight into all aspects of the business?*

Although the VP-HR does not have to be an expert in every arena of the business, she does need to understand the operating approaches of every part of the business. She needs to understand how the pieces should fit together. One of the key roles of HR is to be able to "work at the boundaries" and to make sure that all of the pieces work well together. That will be impossible to do if the VP-HR and others in the HR organization don't really understand how the business components operate and how they are interdependent.

How deep should her understanding be? She should have a basic understanding of the process for financial management. She needs to understand the accounting and budgeting process. She needs to understand the flow of capital and the financial measurement and reporting systems. She needs to understand the flow of product development and manufacturing. She needs to understand the distribution channels, marketing, and sales processes. She needs to understand the high-level governance of the business, including the workings of the board of directors of the organization.

5. *Do I lead in interpreting business strategies into human/organizational implications?*

As I cover in Chapters 6 and 7, it is critical that line management be engaged in the development of the human resources strategy for the organization. However, line managers need to be taught how to make the leap from business issue to human resources issue. The VP-HR, as well as other key HR professionals, must be good at making that leap himself in order to be able to teach it. This jump from business issue to human resources issue has to be second nature. It needs to easily flow off of the tongue of every effective HR leader in the business. This is what will give the line leadership confidence that HR really is interested in the success of the business.

6. Do I set the political context for change?

Change is always a bit unnerving in an organization. There is always significant resistance to change. There are always key leaders who are heavily invested in keeping things exactly as they have always been. If the VP-HR is going to play the key role in the introduction and leadership of change, she must be good at managing the political environment for change, or significant HR change efforts will not be successfully implemented. (Chapter 17 addresses this issue in greater detail.)

7. Can I influence other senior leaders to make the connection between their business needs and human resources solutions?

The effective VP-HR should assume that while most line managers understand that the people aspects of their business are important, they don't know how to intuitively make the connection between business issues and human resources issues. The VP-HR must work with the senior leadership team of the organization, helping them to see how the design of human and organizational processes and systems will help to resolve their business needs. This is best done by centering conversations on the needs of the business leader. The HR leader who cannot help line managers to make that connection will never have their full support, but the HR leader who can will play a critical role in making the line leader a more effective leader.

8. Do I ensure that the organization has the needed resources for change?

Once line leadership and HR agree on a certain direction, HR must be able to assess organizational capabilities against what the change effort will require. The VP-HR must be critical in her assessment. It is easy to fall into the trap of assuming that the organization has all that it needs. Too often, an organization can become incredibly insular in its capabilities, thinking that it is competitive when it is not in fact. The VP-HR also needs to know how to access resources from the outside, from both specialized and traditional resources within the fields of human resources and from line management. HR should be able to source whatever is needed.

9. Do I leverage the junior talent in the HR organization?

The VP-HR needs to be skilled at leveraging the talent that exists inside the organization, as well. I learned a great deal about this as I watched directors of functions reporting to me who were incredibly adept at bringing in junior HR professionals to a complex project, giving them needed training, and then letting them get their hands dirty. Too often, there is a reluctance to give less experienced HR professionals a shot at a piece of work until they've proven their expertise. I have learned that they don't become expert until they get a shot. I have learned to err on the side of letting people jump into the deep end of the pool and giving them lots of coaching as they learn to swim. I discuss this more in Chapter 16.

10. Have I given the HR organization a vision that excites it?

Finally, but perhaps most important, the VP-HR has to give the HR organization a vision that excites it. The VP-HR needs to capture the hearts and imagination of the HR group. This has to be done by providing a compelling picture of how human resources work that is connected to business needs adds value. Most HR professionals are dying for the chance to make a difference to the business. The VP-HR who can give a realistic picture of how they can do that in this organization will win them over.

The VP-HR also needs to model how this is done. She needs to personally lead change and show that she can capture the excitement of line management. Her effectiveness and her reputation for effectiveness will rally her troops behind her.

My experience is that most HR organizations have a segment that is thrilled and freed by a vision of strategic human resources. There is also another segment that is threatened by it. I wish I

could claim that I've learned how to articulate a vision in a way
that excites everyone. I have not. I suspect that is because there
will always be a segment that resists change. So I believe that the
VP-HR leader simply needs to be honest about his vision and the
likely implications that it brings. Channel the energy of those who
love it and help as best you can those who are concerned by it to
manage their concerns.

I am convinced that the position of organizational architect is a wonderful, yet challenging role for someone who can look across all of the
various departmental interests and identify what is needed to improve
the performance of the whole system. The challenge is in helping
management to take that same broad view and not be constrained by
inertia to avoid needed change.

Managing an HR Boss Who Lacks Strategic Focus

Some HR professionals reading this chapter may feel frustrated by
the contrast between the described organizational architect role and
the actual focus of their own senior HR leader. Some challenging
questions for HR professionals include:

- "What do I do if my HR boss is not strategically focused?"
- "How do I become or stay strategic when my HR boss is constantly working on the tactics and expects me to do the same?"

These are difficult situations, hard on personal development and hard
on morale.

Early in my career, I worked for an HR leader who came from a
very traditional, tactical point of view. His power base in the organization seemed to be HR's ability to control policy and certain human
resources processes. I was his director of HR planning and development at the time and was responsible for organization development,

learning and development, and workforce planning. I had gained access to the president of the company in several meetings and had started to feel that he valued my input. He began inviting me to his office to discuss a variety of complex organizational and leadership issues. The president expressed his appreciation for my ability to understand the real business needs and to address them in people and organizational terms. It was clear to me that he wanted to spend more time with me than with my boss, simply because I raised a different level of issues than did my boss. Frankly, I enjoyed these meetings immensely.

My HR boss became increasingly uncomfortable with the attention coming my way from the president. He told me that he expected me to invite him to every meeting that the president asked me to attend. This seemed odd to the president, but he agreed that I should probably do that. I will never forget one day when the two of us were sitting with the president talking through a very complex strategic business issue. The president and I were quite engaged, and it was painfully obvious that my HR boss had little to contribute to the conversation. At one point in the conversation, I could tell that my HR boss was lost and somewhat uncomfortable about the direction of the conversation. He literally kicked me under the table to get me to be quiet and not engage on that topic. I was quite comfortable that the president was engaged and appreciative of the advice that I was giving. I was also clear that my boss was uncomfortable with it, as it represented a fundamentally new philosophical view. That was the day that I decided to leave that particular organization. I was gone within four months.

I wish that I could offer counsel on how to be successful with every boss. I can't. I'm not sure it can be done. In some cases, a strategic HR professional simply has to make an assessment of her ability to be promoted or to wait patiently for the manager's development. I am confident that the marketplace for strategic HR talent is strong enough that no talented HR professional should have to stay in an oppressive environment for long. I do, however, also believe that

HR professionals have an obligation to be patient enough to teach and model a new and more strategic role as best they can. HR leaders who are not strategic themselves should assess their own leadership and decide how they will leverage a talent perhaps unfamiliar to them but increasingly in demand by savvy line leaders.

The same issue exists regarding how to deal with a line leader who is not strategic enough. I know one senior HR leader whose boss retired after years of successful strategic HR efforts that both were fulfilling personally and had great impact on the business. The new line leader took over the reins of the company and made it clear that he saw no reason for HR to be a part of the senior business table. While it was certainly the leader's right to make such a call, this decision left the HR leader with a critical decision. Should he stay in the organization and grow ever more out of touch with the business, or should he leave, allowing the line leader to get an HR leader who would be more inclined to do and enjoy the tactical work that would become his to do? This particular HR leader decided that it was far more important to the field and to him to move on and continue to work with line leaders who were ready to make a difference than to stay in a situation that seemed certain to go backward.

There is a growing cadre of very talented midlevel HR professionals who have an increasing amount of skills and talent to offer. The demand for this type of talent is strong and will continue to grow over time. HR leaders accustomed to a more administrative role should be aware that they can work with and leverage HR professionals who bring different, highly sought-after skills if they only will make the effort. It is a huge opportunity for the next generation of HR leadership, as well as an opportunity for companies that will benefit from the retention of needed talent.

CHAPTER SIX

Clarify Line Management's Role in Creating and Owning Human Resources Strategy

I HAVE HEARD MANY PROFESSIONALS debate the question "Is HR a line management responsibility?" It seems clear to me that "Is it?" is the wrong question. The answer is that it is. General management is responsible for everything that goes on in the organization. It is responsible for marketing, product development, sales, distribution, financial investment and results, and the human and organizational issues. Perhaps better questions include these:

- Is line management serious about people being the company's most important asset?

- Does line management see the connection between human resources and business results?

- Is HR ready to let go of control?

- How do you best engage management?

These are the types of questions that must be addressed to begin to change perspectives around the ownership of human resources work.

For as long as I can remember, HR people have talked about human resources work being line management work. Some businesses have tried to implement that philosophy by structuring themselves along the premise that a company does not need an HR organization. I recall many debates in the 1970s and 1980s over whether part of HR's mission was to work itself out of a job and to hand over the functions of human resources to management and to the employees.

In the extreme, some predicted that all strategic human resources work would go to management or consultants and that all administrative work would be done "self-service" or outsourced or eliminated. Any HR people left would simply be asked to take down the shingle and close up their HR shop.

A notable example of the experimentation with eliminating HR came in the 1980s, when IBM actually moved most of the human resources work outside the corporate organization for a time. Top managers forced themselves to think more carefully about which aspects of human resources work really were needed inside and which ones could be outsourced or eliminated. It seemed incredible that a company as large and complex as IBM would actually outsource HR. This move sent shock waves through the HR community. It was not long, however, before it became clear to those inside IBM that elements of the HR group were missed and had to be brought once again inside the IBM organization. IBM leadership realized that, while it had been bold in its move, it had perhaps gone a bit too far. Many of IBM's strategic partnership and functional HR specialists were brought back inside. The more routine, administrative components remained outside and, in fact, spawned a whole new industry of third-party external HR support companies.

So what did IBM and other companies who followed its example learn? You can't simply get rid of the whole HR function. There are strategic elements of the work that really are best done inside. The strategic components of human resources need to be represented by someone who has regular involvement at the business table. This cannot happen effectively when HR is separated from the business.

But there are many tactical aspects of human resources work that really can be done successfully outside. This was the start of a significant trend to outsourcing administrative portions of human resources work. IBM's action clearly pushed HR in many companies to rethink how the work of human resources would be done in the future.

The Interchange Between Line Management and HR

My experience has been that too few line managers appear eager to get involved in "HR issues." Most seem to wish the people problems would just go away so that they could get on with what they love most—technology, product, sales, and profits. They are happy to have HR "take care of the people stuff." After all, these people issues are complicated, and they are emotional, both for the employee and for the manager. Many line managers are just far more comfortable with their technology than with planning for and resolving people issues.

Many HR folks, on the other hand, act as though line management is just an obstacle in their way, keeping them from implementing some new exciting HR program. They wonder, "Why doesn't management get it? Why can't they see what a great program this is?" Too few HR professionals get involved deeply enough with the customer and business issues to be able to ground their proposals in the business. Many HR proposals are viewed by managers as being self-serving HR forays that may or may not help the business at all. As a result, very few line managers are really involved in setting human resources strategy, and very few HR leaders work hard enough at inviting management into the world of HR. Doesn't this seem odd from coming from a group that is so quick to say that human resources work is line management work?

Cop Versus Partner

I have found it interesting that, while most HR professionals talk about human resources work being the work of management, they often behave as though they really want to keep the work of human resources controlled by the HR function. This way, management has to ask permission of HR. Management has to use HR–designed processes (many of which feel like encumbrances, rather than helpful tools). These processes apply in areas like these:

- Job-level approval

- Compensation limits

- Hiring process

- Policy

What manager has not pulled out his hair fighting with HR on these very issues?

I have vivid memories of specific line managers, red in the face with anger about the restrictions imposed upon them by some HR practice or policy. They seemed to feel powerless to propose processes that would be much more helpful to the business problems they were trying to solve. It feels so often to management that HR's systems are designed more for consistency and ease of implementation for the HR organization than for solving their business concerns.

I am convinced that as long as HR groups continue to maintain primary control in the planning and execution of human resources efforts, they will continue to "push" programs at the line and be frustrated when they meet with objections. They will rarely experience real management "pull" for human resources work.

Clearly, HR's role needs to shift from "cop" to "partner." The cop role means that HR has the power to control management around issues of policy and practice. In far too many organizations, the cop role has simply evolved without good thought being put into the implications of this controlling role. As noted in Figure 6-1, the power base of the cop is one of control rather than competence and expertise. The cop continually tells management what it can and cannot do. Management hates this role. It complains about it, and yet it colludes in it.

Figure 6-1. HR as cop vs. partner.

	Cop	Partner
Power Base	• Sets policy and compliance criteria. • Keeps control.	• Offers expertise and competence. • Has ability to make real business difference.
Objective	• Maintain control. • Provide consistency.	• Foster business growth and success.
Approach	• Provides management with a safety net. • Pushes human resources work.	• Lets management own proposals and be accountable. • Lets management pull human resources work. • Offers consultative persuasion.
Result	• HR becomes an easy target.	• HR and management are partners and co-owners of important human resources work.

Management collusion works something like this: Management knows that the cop is responsible for making sure that the manager doesn't drive himself over the cliff. The HR cop always ensures the safety net and never lets management make a really big mistake. Fair enough. So management's game becomes pushing as close to the edge of the cliff as possible. The manager feels she can do that because, ultimately, HR's job is to keep everybody safe. This allows the manager to push far harder than she otherwise would; the HR safety net will always be there to catch her. This is a game where neither HR nor line management is behaving like an adult.

Engaging Management

We must move beyond talking about HR being the work of management and begin behaving as though we mean it. So how can we truly engage line management? It certainly begins with effective partnership between senior-level HR generalists and line management.

One of my first questions as I joined Hallmark was "How can HR start walking the talk about management owning human resources work?" As in many organizations, I could see a lot of rhetoric but little action on either HR's or the line's part to suggest that people really meant what they were saying. I didn't want to continue playing the cop game. I decided that I had to develop a philosophy and real-world practices that suggested that I believed that human resources work really is management work.

I worked with the CEO as I struggled to come up with an approach that would solve the problem. Slowly, it dawned on me that if I wanted line management to own human resources work, it needed to own human resources work. Though it may seem very simple—obvious, in fact—I, like most other HR leaders, had spent my whole career assuming that I would develop proposals for human resources direction and then try to sell them to management. This whole paradigm had to be blown up and redone. We needed to design a way for management, in fact, to actually own human resources work. It needed to own the processes, the plan, the decisions, and the results. The strategic direction for people and organizational issues should be management's decision, not HR's.

Using Corporate Committees

So what does it look like when management is in control of and owns human resources work? How does it work? My answer is grounded in the work of strategic human resources. It starts with moving from the business plan to the HR Plan (HRP). At Hallmark, I proposed the development of six corporate human resources committees that would reflect the five processes of the human resources model and a diversity committee that already existed in the company. Such an approach is depicted in Figure 6-2.

Before getting into the details of this particular approach, let me outline the principles that are at its base. They are these:

Figure 6-2. Management of human resources committees.

Corporate HR Committee:		
Chair:	CEO	
Members:	President	
	VP of HR	
	Meet - 2x/year	

ER/Policy Committee	Performance Management Committee	Learning & Development Committee	Organization Development Committee	Workforce Planning & Staffing Committee	Diversity Committee
Chair: Corporate Officer	Chair: Corporate Officer	Chair: Corporate Officer	Chair: Corporate Officer	Chair: Corporate Officer	Chair: Corporate Officer
Facilitator: Dir-Employee Relations	Facilitator: Dir-Performance Mgmt & Rewards	Facilitator: Dir-Learning & Development	Facilitator: Dir-Org Development	Facilitator: Dir-Workforce Planning	Facilitator: Dir-Diversity
Line Manager Line Manager Line Manager Line Manager	Line Manager Line Manager Line Manager Line Manager	Line Manager Line Manager Line Manager Line Manager	Line Manager Line Manager Line Manager Line Manager	Line Manager Line Manager Line Manager Line Manager	*Corporate Diversity Council Members*
HR Manager HR Manager	HR Manager HR Manager	HR Manager HR Manager	HR Manager HR Manager	HR Manager HR Manager	

Functional HR Committees

Meet - 4x/year

- Human resources work is line management work.

- Line and HR should work together on human resources strategy.

- Human resources strategy should be aligned with the business strategy. It is really a chapter of the business plan.

- Line leaders should be involved in the development of human resources strategy, and it should be theirs. They get the final say.

- Line leaders propose the human resources strategy to the CEO.

- HR's power base is not the ability to control information and compensation. It is its "technical expertise" regarding people and organization issues. HR contributes the best available human resources insight on processes, tools, and methods.

- Management should not design human resources tactics. HR specialists do that.

- If HR disagrees with a direction that the line wants to take, HR owes the company an expert point of view. This is HR's "audit role." HR understands, however, that management has the final say.

- Component HR plans should be integrated at various levels in the organization.

- Line "pulls" human resources work. HR never "pushes" human resources work.

- Line management is responsible for implementation of the HRP.

- HR professionals serve as technical advisers to management in the development of the HRP.

- HR plays the key role in the process and program management of implementing the HRP.

In the approach depicted in Figure 6-2, each committee was chaired by a line officer of the company. The chairs would rotate about every three years. These committees were accountable to the CEO—not to HR—to develop the human resources strategy. These HR strategies were to be directly aligned with the business strategy. Who should know the business strategy better than the corporate officers?

For example, the officer chair of the organization development committee was responsible for taking the business strategy and translating it into the appropriate organization development strategy for the company. In other words, he would determine what the company should do in the organization development arena in order to successfully support the business strategy. The officer chair of the performance management committee was responsible for taking the business strategy and translating it into the appropriate performance management strategy for the corporation. Each committee was set up in the same manner.

Each committee was also facilitated by the HR director of that particular HR group. All of those directors reported to me. Membership on the committees was made up primarily of senior and influential line management. Each committee also had the needed HR technical experts to contribute their expertise to the identified work.

These committees met three to five times annually to do their work. The meetings were kept at a very high and strategic level. They were not to dip down into the tactical elements of implementation. Surprisingly, I learned that some line leaders wanted to meet more often as they enjoyed having greater influence in the human resources arena.

How the Committee Process Flowed

Ideally, committee meetings each year went something like this:

First meeting:	Review the business strategy and begin thinking about the human resources implications.
Second meeting:	Brainstorm specific human resources implications of the business strategies. Prioritize those that are of greatest value to the organization.
Third meeting:	Finalize the proposal for that committee's area to be passed on to the CEO. On the basis of the CEO's acceptance of the proposal, assign subgroups to do research and design on these solutions.
Fourth meeting:	Review and assess actual accomplishments against last year's plan.

How often did it work exactly this way? Rarely. Every committee had a different personality. One line leader got so into his committee dealing with incentive issues that the group met at least monthly. We were more than happy to let it do so. Spending all that time built the level of commitment to the proposals that came out of that committee.

Each year the committee chair gave the committee's plan to me, and I integrated all of the plans into a preliminary human resources strategy proposal for the company. The plans also came with an analysis of resources needed to accomplish what was proposed: money, time, management focus, and so on. We were clear that the company would not be able to do everything that was proposed—there would never be enough resources. However, we wanted to make sure that executive leadership understood the full array of options available to it to support its business strategy. From these options, it could make informed decisions.

I merged all of the input into a format that allowed analysis. My role was not to interpret or change the input. It was simply to consolidate the committee work into a format that could be reviewed by the CEO. My staff then took several weeks with this raw input to organize it into a proposed HR Plan. We never made decisions as to what would stay in or be cut. We were very clear that those calls were the responsibility of the line.

We did, however, want to arrive at an HR point of view that I would share with the CEO. This was HR's final opportunity to let the CEO and other leaders know of any concerns that HR had with the plan and/or our level of support. By the time the plans reached this stage, however, there were generally few surprises or profound differences of opinion between management and HR. After all, HR had been working with the line on these over the course of a year.

I then met with the CEO and other appropriate executive leadership to make final determinations. As we dealt with each committee's proposal, we assessed the organization's ability to accomplish the plan and then prioritized the components into the final strategic HRP for the company. We reviewed it in its completed form with the management team so that everyone knew exactly what HR's agenda was for the coming year. Ultimately, it was the CEO's plan, not mine. It was recommended to him by his key line executives, not by HR.

Eliminating the Need to "Push" HR Plans

Now we were starting to "hardwire" management into the human resources process. Line leaders didn't just have a point of view. They didn't just review HR proposals. They owned them! These were their priorities. It was wonderful to deal with a plan that had line leadership's support. Of course it was supported—it was theirs.

When human resources strategy is developed this way, the role of HR changes dramatically. HR is no longer pushing programs at the line but running to keep up with the human resources strategies developed by management. That is a high-class problem for HR.

I find far too many HR groups working far too hard to develop proposals to management for initiatives with which management is not familiar. This makes human resources work far too easy for the line. It has little skin in the game. It doesn't have to make any commitment to the effort until the very end. It can wait to read the political tea leaves as the proposal progresses and then at the last minute make a personal decision about its level of support. Too frequently, by that time the decision is based more on the politics of the day than on a heartfelt commitment that this is the right thing for the company. When a corporate officer has done the groundwork—even made the proposal to the CEO himself—the politics are largely taken out. Line leaders propose only what they already back. The success rate of these proposals is far greater than those for which HR groups have created the majority of the proposals on their own.

The Process in Action

It may be helpful to use an example and show the mechanics of how this really works. Let's assume a given business has the following four points as central to its strategy:

- Broaden the number of business platforms.
- Cut costs.
- Acquire new distribution.
- Strengthen product quality.

Each of the committees is responsible for proposing the human resources plan for a specific area of responsibility in support of these four strategic directions.

The workforce planning and staffing committee, for example, might ask the following questions for each of the four business strategy areas:

- What are the implications of this strategy for the workforce?
- What skills are we likely to need more of? Less of?
- How much more or less? In what time frame?
- Where will these people come from? Inside? Outside? How will we source this talent?
- What will be the financial implications of this sourcing?
- Do we need new leadership skills? Do we have them inside?
- Will we have people that are no longer needed? What will we do with them?
- Will we need a placement strategy? Will attrition take care of it?

Against this assessment, the committee will propose specific actions to be taken by the company to fulfill the workforce and staffing needs. It will identify the resources needed to fulfill these plans. Now it will have a plan ready to be merged with the other committees' work, creating a foundation for the company's HRP.

As a result of that business strategy, the learning and development committee might ask the following questions:

- What new skills will be needed?
  - Technical or domain skills
  - Management skills
  - Leadership skills
- How many people with these skills do we have inside the organization, and can they be made available?
  - What does the succession plan tell us?
  - Do we have an adequate talent review process?

- How might we develop these skills?
  - Work on committees
  - Work assignment with peers
  - Mentors
  - Coaches
  - Programs
  - New job assignment

The organization development committee might ask questions that include the following:

- What will be the impact of these strategic directions on the work processes of the company?
- How will decisions be made?
- What impact will these changes have on the control processes of the company?
- What impact will they have on the communications processes of the company?
- How do we want to organize these new business platforms?
- How will we organize these new distribution channels?
- What impact might the cost focus have upon the organization?
  - Will we consolidate functions?
  - Will we create a central services organization?
- What are the implications to the overall corporate governance?

The performance management committee might consider the following implications for that arena of work:

- What are the objectives and metrics for each of these new organizational entities?
- How will we flow these measures down throughout the organization?

- What can we do to make sure that we manage organizations and individuals to these metrics?

- Does the performance review process help or get in the way of these new strategic directions?

- How should we think about the incentive pay systems for these new businesses?

- Can these new businesses carry the same employee cost load as our core businesses?

- Will the core business benefits programs work with cost models from the new businesses?

On the basis of that business strategy, the employee relations committee might pose questions that include these:

- What will be the employee reaction to these structural and business changes?

- How will these changes impact the general sense of employee agreement that we currently have with employees?

- How do we want to communicate these changes to the employees?

- Why should the average employee support these changes?

Finally, some potential questions the diversity committee might raise as a result of that strategy are these:

- What opportunities will these new structures provide for leadership and other positions for women and people of color?

- Will there be any adverse impact upon employees as a result of these changes?

- How will we deal with the fundamentally different cultures that will be a part of these new businesses?

- How will we integrate the different points of view held by different functions in the business?

These questions outline a basic approach for the inclusion of management in the formation of the HRP. A more detailed description of the creation of the HRP is found in Chapter 7.

In summary, the process steps are as follows:

1. Individual human resources committees review and understand the business strategy. They are led by a corporate officer who was part of the original development of the business strategy.

2. Human resources committees meet as needed to interpret the business plan into a proposal for a specific area of HR. They identify resources needed to fulfill this plan and they prioritize aspects of the proposal.

3. Proposals from all committees are integrated and formatted into a final draft of the company HRP.

4. The CEO, VP-HR, and other executives review the proposal and finalize the HRP.

5. Committees assess the effectiveness of last year's plan.

Lingering Questions

Several questions that regularly come up regarding this approach are worth consideration. They include these:

1. *How did you get line management to be willing to do this?*

   It actually was easy. The involvement of the CEO was a critical element. It is crucial that this philosophy of management ownership and involvement be held at the top. If it isn't, it will be difficult at best to engage the most senior leaders in human resources planning and work.

We started by having a joint proposal from the CEO and the VP-HR. I was fortunate. It was clear that Hallmark's CEO supported this approach and was willing to let the management team know that. I remember telling him in my initial recruiting interview that I assumed that he was the key people leader of the company, not me. I told him that if he was hiring me to take all of the people issues off of his plate so that he could get on with the more important business work, I was clearly the wrong person for the job and that he should keep looking.

Even more important than the support of the CEO at Hallmark was the fact that this was the first time for many leaders to actually have the chance to strongly influence aspects of human resources work. Up to this time, they had felt overly controlled by the HR group. Now HR was actually letting them into the inner sanctum and inviting them to play. They loved it. I will never forget the line leader who said, "You mean I get to set the direction for compensation here?" The answer was yes, that was exactly what we meant. He did go forward and set the most progressive changes to a performance-based compensation plan that the company had ever seen. I am convinced that this plan would not have been accepted if the HR group had made the exact same proposal. It was accepted because key line leaders said that they needed it. Once management understood this, it was quite enthusiastic about participating.

2. How did HR maintain control?

We didn't. HR leadership cannot try this approach until it is ready to stop controlling management. The power base assumed in this approach shifts from control to competence and influence. Control over management has been a power base for HR for too long. The field has far too many leaders who know no other way to have power than to control policy and rewards. Ultimately, this is illegitimate power. These systems belong to the organization and not to HR. Management should have access to and control of any and all human resources systems.

This approach requires HR professionals—and especially HR leaders—to have self-confidence in their ability to participate in the business dialogue and then to contribute in a meaningful way to the development of the HR Plan. It requires leaders who have come to understand influence by expertise, not control.

3. How did HR ensure that the right things were being done?

HR provides technical expertise in areas of human resources design. It should know best practices and have a strong point of view about how to apply the best theory and practice to the specific needs of the business. At any and every point of the process of developing and implementing the HRP, HR professionals should make their perspective clear. Ideally, they will have effective enough influence skills that they can guide management to the best approaches.

My experience is that, once management owns human resources work, it becomes much more appreciative of HR professionals' technical skills. It learns how hard human resources work really is. I found that it relies on and values HR's point of view more, not less, when HR lets go of control. It starts to truly act as a partner with HR.

HR people often ask, "What if management wants to do something really dumb and/or illegal? What do we do then?" I tried to be very clear with line leaders that if I ever felt that they were proposing something that was either dumb or illegal, I would let them know. I feel that this is the "fiduciary" responsibility of HR. That is different, however, from saying that I won't let them do something.

If line leaders feel strongly enough about the proposal to take it to the CEO despite my concerns, I want them to know that I also will let the CEO know that in my opinion she is about to see a proposal that from an HR technical point of view I consider to be dumb or illegal. If they feel strongly enough to move forward against the technical advice of HR, so be it. They control the policy, not HR. At that point, the HR leader has a choice. If this is a big enough deal to him that he cannot be associated with the company's doing whatever is being proposed, he can quit. If it is a preference or stylistic difference but not one that violates deep personal values, he may simply let it go.

I have found that most line managers don't intend to do anything to the business that is dumb or illegal. The scenario I have described is highly unlikely. My experience and belief is that line managers usually want what's best for the organization. I have actually found them to become quite conservative in their proposals once they realized that they have the final call. They are not looking to see how far they can push the "HR cop." They have an HR partner who will support their ultimate decision. I cannot overemphasize the shift that needs to happen in HR groups to a new power base of technical competence and the ability to influence.

4. Does this mean that HR and line management agree on everything?

Of course not. HR and the line still have serious debates. They disagree on many things. This disagreement is healthy and serves to keep everybody honest. What is clear is how the differences will be resolved. At the strategic level, line management sets and owns the agenda. It can manage human resources issues however it chooses. HR provides a clear and strong technical voice.

The tension between line and HR perspectives can be a healthy tension. We often view the world from different angles, which means that there will be differences of opinion. In addition to HR's needing to let go of control, line management needs to learn how to effectively debate critical human resources issues in an open and straightforward way. I have known key line leaders who have been uncomfortable with the technical debate raised by an HR group or HR leader. The process I describe assumes that the line leader is open to—in fact, encourages—a good debate on the differences in perspective. If he is not able to foster a dialogue with differences of opinion, this approach will not likely work.

5. *How did you integrate the work of the various committees?*

For the most part, these committees worked separately. There were several points of integration, however, including these:

- HR leaders who were part of each committee were also part of the senior HR staff. The HR staff had regular conversations about the work of the committees, particularly if work in one seemed incompatible with that in another.

- During the business planning time frame, the HR staff collected all of the committee's proposals and integrated their formats. It also highlighted the key questions and issues for the executive review of the plan.

- Finally, all of this work was integrated when the CEO and VP-HR sat together with other senior leaders to finalize the HRP.

As the VP-HR, I had to be regularly engaged in what was going on in these committees. I checked in with them by:

- Training them initially on their roles and what was expected of them

- Attending as many of their meetings as possible

- Staying in touch with the HR leaders on the teams to know where they were going directionally

- Giving them my thoughts on a regular basis as to how this work might be approached

These points of integration may or may not be enough. Each organization should think about points of integration that will work best in its culture.

6. *Did all of the committees at Hallmark work equally well?*

Absolutely not. I would say that about half worked very well and half were OK but could have been much better. Those that worked well did so because line management got truly engaged and had passion for the work that it was doing. The committees worked well when the HR functional leader caught the vision and was effectively working behind the scenes to influence and support the line manager, helping him to be successful. I was constantly reminded that engaging management in human resources strategy takes a lot of ongoing effort.

7. So, having done this, what did you learn?

The learning comes both from things that worked and from things that didn't. I would follow this procedure again in any company. If senior leaders were not interested enough to spend four days a year to identify the people strategy for the company, I'd find another organization that knows how to use my talent.

Some points to keep in mind:

- Not all managers understand human resources work. Many assume that it is simple and for whatever reason don't want to be bothered with it.

- Many HR people really can't let go of control. They haven't learned to influence. They don't understand the business enough to have confidence playing in the business arena.

- A few managers feel that HR is abdicating its responsibility by using this approach. Interestingly, one of the leaders who was most involved in his leadership of a committee—the group that met most frequently—later became frustrated that he was doing too much of HR's work. Hard to have it both ways. (I discuss this more in Chapter 17.)

- When it comes time for the strategies to be judged as successful or not, HR may still be left holding the bag. When one strategy was not ultimately supported by the senior leadership of the company, there was no line management in sight. Some dynamics may never change.

- A big problem that still exists is the need to develop measurement systems for tracking the progress of the human resources work comparable to the systems used to track other business issues.

Can This Method Work in All Organizations?

Not necessarily this specific approach. Every organization has its own culture, history, and way of doing things. Implementation of these principles will be different in every organization. The principles are what matters, not the specific applications of them.

Alternatives to the Committee Approach

While the six-committee approach used at Hallmark worked in that environment, it will not work in every environment. It is important to realize that the message here is about principles, not about structure. I have worked with a variety of companies that have implemented committees in concept but had to adapt the structure to fit their specific circumstances.

Here are some alternative approaches that have proved successful.

Alternative 1. One particular company did not deal well with committees. It chose to have only one senior-level committee made up of top management and the VP-HR. Rather than having multiple committees, it had one committee with multiple agendas. It then used a group as a sounding board, a cross-functional team of line and HR leaders that reacted to and critiqued the directions that the committee was proposing. This alternative approach is depicted in Figure 6-3.

Alternative 2. Another large, complex global organization put together a team of six key line management leaders and gave it the task of identifying the most important human resources issues in the organization. The group did this by going through a process very similar to the one defined in Chapter 7 for developing an HRP. Once these three areas were identified, it created a committee for each area. These three committees were chaired by one of the line leaders and populated with internal HR leaders, as well as some external content experts. These committees worked to-

Figure 6-3. The HR advisory council.

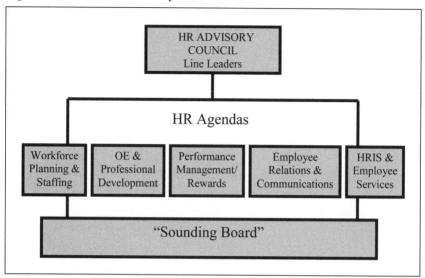

gether to propose the specific human resources tools and processes that were needed in order to effect the needed change. Once again, this is simply another way line management can play the key role in determining the human resources strategy and then working with HR in doing the actual design work that is needed.

Alternative 3. With yet another company that was set against any use of committees, the head of HR and I interviewed each officer. We asked them these questions:

• What are your customer needs?

• How well are you meeting these needs as demonstrated by your business results?

• What is your strategy?

• What are the human resources implications of that strategy?

The head of HR and I then summarized all of the input and brought it forward to the president and the management team to finalize what the HR Plan should be. As a team, they identified three strategic human resources efforts that became the core of the HRP. In essence, the leadership team became the committee. It identified and therefore owned the human resources priorities of the company.

Alternative 4. Another organization designed a large two-day workshop that brought forty key line and HR leaders together. They identified the business environment, the optimal strategy, and the specific human resources efforts that would support that strategy. They did a nice job of making sure that the plan was owned by line management and of aligning HR and management around the specific human resources needs of the company.

What Is the Best Approach for Your Organization?

In determining the best approach to take in a given organization, it may be helpful for you to consider this question: Where is cross-level, cross-functional work most effectively accomplished in this organization? In committees? One on one? In staff work, where groups are given a particular assignment that forces them to go across the organization? Or in some other forum?

After determining that, then identify options for engaging management in human resources strategy development and implementation. You might decide on one of these venues or choose something else altogether:

- Set up committees at a corporate level.

- Set up committees at a division level.

- Set up consolidated committees.

- Have top management team establish all human resources plans together.

- Have HR propose the plan for management review and approval.

- Have a business strategy process create the HRP.

Executive line and HR leadership should then choose the best option for the particular organization. Again, the principles are the key to effective management engagement, but there are many different approaches that could work.

Applying These Principles Throughout the Organization

These principles can and should apply on multiple levels. A strong HR partner at an entry level of the organization must ask the same questions as are asked at the top of the house, including these:

- How can I contribute to the development of the business strategy and goals at my level of the organization?
- How do I engage my managers in the development of the human resources strategy for our level of the HR organization?
- How do I ensure that line management makes the final proposals and decisions on the HRP? How do I ensure that management feels a sense of ownership for the HRP?

Take, for example, an HR business partner working in a manufacturing plant with a group of a few hundred employees and a management team consisting of a manager with seven supervisors. Just as he would be at the top of the organization, this HR professional should be engaged in the development of the strategy for that particular manufacturing line. He could facilitate a leadership session for the manager where the strategy is interpreted into a human resources plan for the group. The decisions, however, would be made by the management team. Another option is to form a subset of the management team in combination with key employees of the organization and have them determine the human resources work that needs to be done. Once again, the format is far less important than the principles.

A Successful Partnership

It may be helpful to review the attributes and action needed by HR and by line management to achieve effective people and organizational management. A true HR business partner has these qualities:

- Is first a business leader who works "people issues"
- Has a clear business point of view
- Participates fully in the development of strategy
- Interprets strategy into a full range of people and organizational implications
- Ensures availability of necessary resources
- Leads the successful design and implementation of programs, processes, and tools that lead to the achievement of business strategy
- Identifies and leads significant change efforts
- Takes and manages risk
- Measures success by impact upon the business

A line manager effectively engaged in human resources work displays these qualities:

- Walks and talks the talk about people issues.
- Is willing to devote time to working on people issues.
- Intuitively sees the people implications of business strategies.
- Sees the value of process as a means to an end.
- Is personally able to do the hard people management issues well.
- Manages performance.
- Differentiates performance and pay.
- Develops self and others to deliver excellence.

CHAPTER SEVEN

Create a Human and Organizational Strategy

IN MY CONSULTING WORK, when I meet with a client and ask to see the HR Plan (HRP), more often than not I receive a document that has been developed by the HR department for the HR department and likely has had only modest review from line management. It simply describes the work of the HR department. One such HRP was meticulously written under the following general headings:

- Executive Summary (a description of the role, structure, and charter of the HR department)

- The HR department's objectives and historical background

- An assessment of the HR department's strengths and weaknesses

- Strategic initiatives of the HR department (e.g., medical plan enrollment, open enrollment, drug testing, job family design, employment department needs, automation of the hiring and termination process, employee survey, sales training, update to the personnel manual, and a computer system upgrade)

Now, this just doesn't feel like a strategic list of work that is linked at all with the company's strategy. And, in this particular company, it wasn't. These efforts may all be useful things to do. But they are not at the center of work that will enable the corporate strategy to meet the needs of paying customers.

In other organizations, I get a document that has obviously been begrudgingly developed by an administrative assistant, following a preset format and having very little real thought behind it. Someone was told that to do a HR Plan by filling in the blanks of a form. Of course, none of these approaches is consistent with the principles described in Chapter 6 on management involvement.

What Is a Human Resources Plan (HRP)?

The HRP is the component of the business plan that makes clear the aspects of people and organization in your business that are critical to meeting your strategy, satisfying your customers, and motivating them to buy your product or services. It clarifies what will be done in a given time frame and who will do it.

Difference Between the Company's HRP and the HR Department Plan

The company's HR Plan is the company's people and organization plan. It should be thought of as a chapter of the overall business plan, a parallel chapter to other chapters dealing with technology, product, market, and investment. It aligns with the business plan and is owned by the senior line leader. HR participates in its development and implementation.

The HR Department Plan is the "business plan" of the HR department. I call it that having considered the classical definition of a business plan. Imagine that the HR department is really "HR Inc.," with customers, products and services, and a budget. HR Inc. needs a plan that aligns its vision/purpose with its strategy, capabilities, and tactical plans. It is derived from the company's HRP, and HR typically project-manages most of it. It reflects HR's commitment to its cus-

tomer: line management. The HR Department Plan ensures that resources are available to implement the HRP:

- People (internal and external)
- Money
- Management time and attention

Its purpose is to support the HRP, and it usually identifies tactics
necessary to fulfill the strategies in the HRP.

The Starting Point Is the Business Plan—If There Is One

If the HR Plan is derived from the organization's business plan or
strategy, the organization's business plan would seem an easy place
to start. But it is not as easy as it might sound. Frankly, in some
organizations it is difficult to get ahold of the business strategy, and,
even if you do, it is often not very strategic. If you ask for the "business plan" in any given organization, you might receive any of the
following documents:

- The overall business strategy (if the organization has one)
- The budget
- The performance measurement plan
- The marketing plan
- The product plan

Far too often, business plans are simply a description of goals (e.g.,
achieve x percent ROA), rather than a strategy that makes clear the
overall direction for the organization and what will make it win in the
marketplace.

I have always thought of business strategy as having the following
dimensions:

- Strategy is about directional choices made from various alternatives as to how you might focus and run your business. There are many alternatives. Your strategy reflects your choices and makes it clear what you are choosing to do, as well as what you are not choosing to do.

- A strategy should be selected because leadership believes these particular choices will provide competitive advantage to win in the marketplace.

- Good strategies are clear enough that all employees can interpret direction for their specific work from these defined strategies.

- Goals are not strategies. Goals reflect what you want to achieve. Strategies reflect how you plan to achieve them.

The HR Plan will be only as strategic as the business plan.

When the Overall Business Strategy Is Weak

Strategic human resources can't really exist in an organization that doesn't have a clear and viable strategy linked directly to customer needs. Where there is no clear or effective business strategy, there is an opportunity for the VP-HR to demonstrate his worth and to facilitate discussions with the CEO and the senior leadership team to produce a strategy that is more precise, more effective, and/or more focused on the customer. HR leaders can raise the questions that help others to recognize where a strategy is unclear or ineffective. Top leadership needs to produce a business plan that articulates a strategy, a clear set of choices of how that organization will win in the marketplace. Too many business leaders have developed "strategies" that reflect the internal interests or abilities of leaders (often technology and product leaders), rather than the external interests of real customers.

Early in my career, I was fascinated by the struggle that I saw in many leadership groups to develop a clear strategy. I became convinced that, in part, the struggle existed because of the different points of view with which leaders entered the strategic conversation. I found three different perspectives generally taken by leaders involved in strategy development. I came to realize how profoundly these different perspectives can influence a strategic conversation and the roles people play. These perspectives are represented in Figure 7-1.

Some leaders come from the perspective of planning for "what I

Figure 7-1. Leadership perspectives.

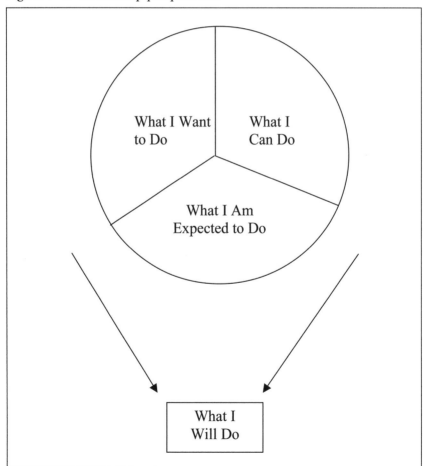

want to do." These are the great visionaries of the team. They have great ideas, and they can see forever, but they may be short on specifics and implications. Others come from the perspective of "what I can do." These are the more conservative people who have to be sure that they have every resource lined up before they take the risk to set up a plan. They will never commit to something that they are not sure they can accomplish. These are the sandbaggers. Finally, others enter the strategic discussion from the perspective of doing "what I am expected to do." These may be the expectations they anticipate from the CEO, the board, or whomever. These are the pleasers. They are driven to meet the expectations of others.

In any group working on strategy, there are people in the room who represent each of these views. Obviously, these three differing perspectives will lead to very different ultimate strategies. So which of these three points of view is the right one from which to develop the best strategy? None of them! They are all problematic if they are the only point of view expressed or considered. Blue-sky leaders with no constraints have taken whole organizations right off the cliff with their unconstrained wishes, hopes, and dreams. On the other hand, the sandbaggers would never have the courage to make the first step into the fray of a real business environment. And those who want to make others happy may say "yes" to everything with no sense of the realities of how to actually accomplish the work. They won't propose a daring or cutting-edge strategy because they are aiming only to do what is already expected of them.

An effective strategy development team has voices from each of these perspectives in the strategic discussion. They balance one another nicely. Each is needed. So what does this have to do with HR? Having HR at the table greatly increases the likelihood that these dynamics will be identified and managed to make sure that the best strategy is developed. HR can be hugely helpful to the team in its strategy development process. (For excellent resources on strategy development, see the Appendix.)

Creating an HRP

How does one approach developing an HRP? Figure 7-2 presents a framework that I have used to help many organizations develop their HR Plan. It suggests that the HRP start with descriptions of the strategic directions of the organization. In starting here, I assume that the strategy of the organization is directly linked to the needs of customers. If not, the HR leader should start by refocusing the strategic conversation to make sure that it is grounded in real customer needs.

What are the specific market strategies that your organization is pursuing? Write them across the top of the diagram. Each of these strategic directions is then translated into its implications for each of the five human resources processes and diversity. Once the entire matrix has been filled out, the horizontal rows represent the company's plan for a given functional aspect of human resources (e.g., organization development or learning and development). The vertical columns represent all that needs doing from a human resources standpoint to support that particular aspect of the business plan. The totality of the diagram represents all of the possible efforts that might be initiated to support the business plan.

Figure 7-2. Developing the HR strategy.

	Broaden Business Platforms	Cut Costs	Acquire Distribution	Strengthen Product	Other	
Workforce Planning & Staffing						
Learning & Development						
Orgnization Development						
Performance Management						
Employee Relations						
Diversity						

As an example, a business plan might include the need to move into new lines of business through acquisitions. In creating an HRP from that strategy, what are the strategic human resources implications of such a business plan? Here are some possibilities:

Workforce Planning and Staffing. Moving into new or different lines of business through acquisitions usually requires that leaders possess skill sets and expertise different from what was essential in the core business. And so this business strategy drives the need to attract, integrate, and retain leaders with those different skill sets. Future plans to assimilate newly acquired companies and to eliminate the redundancies that inevitably exist have a substantial impact on workforce planning, particularly in the areas of retention and placement.

At Hallmark Cards, we knew that we had the world's best talent in the area of cards, but as we ventured into new businesses it became clear that we needed to hire new talent—particularly new leaders—that understood these different marketplaces and how to succeed in them. Previous attempts to succeed in new businesses through leaders who at their core were card people just had not worked. We needed people who understood a whole new business approach.

Organization Development. Acquiring other companies raises questions about the larger design of the organization. How will the corporation treat acquisitions? What is the expected cultural and capabilities fit between the companies? Does the company want to become a tightly integrated corporation? Or is it more interested in pursuing a holding company strategy and configuration? How much independence should there be between the core business and the newly acquired business? How similar are the business models of the core company and the new businesses? Whatever the decision, there will need to be some critical linkages established between companies. This must become a key component of the HRP.

Performance Management. Acquired companies usually bring with them different performance management practices. Often the whole culture of performance management is different. Integration of these different systems is often very complicated and requires extensive work. The implications may be insignificant for the general employee population, depending on how closely linked and how consistent practices need to be between the core business and the acquired companies. However, at a higher leadership level, expectations, metrics, and rewards most likely will need to be determined for the management team of the acquired corporation.

Employee Relations. Acquisitions—no matter what the philosophy of integration is—always involve employee relations issues. How will we deal with employees' questions about the acquisition, the impact upon the company, and the impact upon them personally? The HRP should spell out a recommended plan for how to deal with employee concerns throughout this transition.

Learning and Development. As you bring in a newly acquired company, there will likely be extensive development needed to make sure that new managers understand the new philosophy and management practices. They often need training in key aspects of the new marketplace. The HRP should clarify all of these needs for development.

Prioritizing Work to Resources

In almost every case, a fully completed matrix offers up more work than an organization is capable of completing. It is critical to prioritize which suggestions actually can and should be targeted for completion. Available resources are always limited, and management must determine which of all these recommendations will actually have resources put against them. If the company is using a human resources committee process, the leaders of each committee should prioritize their specific proposals. The CEO, president, and VP-HR then make a final prioritization of the proposals and commit resources to accomplish these proposals.

Finding a Useful Format

Related to the need to prioritize, it is equally important to put the HRP into a format that can be easily understood and communicated. We discovered that lengthy, detailed versions of the HRP simply didn't work. Our first versions of the HRP were five to seven pages long. They were simply too long and too detailed; no one read the plan and stayed focused on it. We had to find a way to shorten it.

Once all of the items are prioritized, HR and management can identify the two to four core human resources themes that are reflected in the recommendations. I found that if we summarized two to four themes on a single page, management was able to stay focused on the human resources direction for the company. It is critical that this plan be marketed in a way that is easy to digest and understand. An example of such a summary is offered in Figure 7-3.

My intent with this example was to take a rather complex listing of potential human resources issues that needed our attention and to simplify them. You might take the myriad human resource efforts identified and identify two to four themes into which they can all be

Figure 7-3. Sample human resources plan.

Vision: The right workforces in the right environments delivering profitable business growth.		
Our HR vision will be accomplished by focusing on three broad initiatives:		
WORKFORCE PLANNING	**LEADERSHIP**	**GROWTH & PERFORMANCE**
Scope and Focus ❑ **Workforce Reduction** • Ensure that we have the needed consistent with business models and current financial plans. ❑ **Retention** • Improve retention and take a strong employee advocacy position to ensure the engagement of the desired workforce. ❑ **Recruiting and Development** • Identify needed skill mix changes. • Upgrade talent where needed.	*Scope and Focus* ❑ **Change Management** • Develop effective change plans. • Link change skill development to specific business needs and target those who need it. ❑ **Targeted Senior Management Development** • Link to specific business needs and target leaders who need it; to be linked business model timing. ❑ **Succession Planning** • Continue rollout of process and tools across the enterprise. ❑ **Management/Supervisory Development** • Continue skill development based on Gallup best practices. • Upgrade managers' ability to motivate, for, and differentiate.	*Scope and Focus* ❑ **Effective design and implementation of Business Models within and across businesses** ❑ **Performance Management & Total Reward Systems for the Corporation** • Complete executive compensation realignment. • Develop and implement an integrated performance measurement system. ❑ **Continue Implementation of Global Shared Services**

placed. Keeping the plan this simple allows leaders to keep the HR plan top of mind.

The example given of how to translate strategy into an HRP is the process that we used at Hallmark Cards and that has been successfully used at a variety of other companies. The advantages of this approach are that it is relatively simple and that it connects the eventual HRP to the company's strategy for meeting customer needs.

Ensuring an Effective HRP

In summary, what are the principles for human resources planning? They include these points:

- The HRP is a subcomponent of the business plan.

- The HRP is driven by the business strategy.

- Line managers should identify key HRP components and directions at the highest level.

- HR provides the technical roadmap, or HR Department Plan, for accomplishing the HRP.

- HR consults on the technical and legal appropriateness of the HRP.

- Line management has the final decision on the HRP.

- You can't do everything; prioritize what is most important and where you can actually make a difference.

- Once the organization's HRP is developed, the HR department can create its department business plan that indicates what HR will do in support of the HRP.

By assessing which of these principles are most lacking in an HR planning process, HR leaders can target areas of improvement to make planning much more effective.

CHAPTER EIGHT

Examine the Five Human Resources Processes Through a Strategic Lens

"There are no rules here. We're just trying to accomplish something."

—THOMAS EDISON

IN CHAPTER 4, I introduced a model reproduced here as Figure 8-1, which depicts the relationship among the marketplace, the business strategy, human talent, and human resources work. It identifies five human resources processes that have proven to be a useful categorization for me. In the five chapters that follow (Chapters 9–13), I examine the five human resources processes in greater detail and explore what strategic work in each of these arenas looks like. I am providing not an in-depth treatise on each of these processes but some examples, principles, and learnings that HR professionals can apply to their own particular situations.

HR leaders commonly make the mistake of viewing these five areas as HR organizational units and not as work processes. Although the units of an HR organization may well be designed along the lines of these processes, I am here again much more interested in the work of human resources than in the structure of an HR organization. I address the design of the HR organization in Chapter 15.

Some would ultimately choose to categorize human resources

Figure 8-1. Strategic human resources framework.

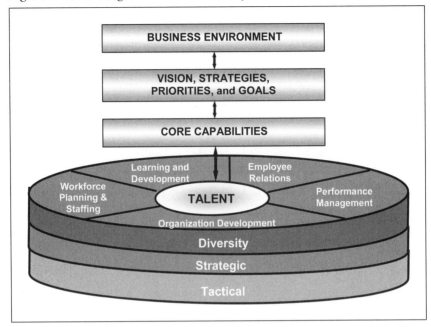

work differently. Again, my particular model is not the key; what is important is having a clear framework that is based on human resources work, rather than on HR organizational boxes.

What Work Do the Five Processes Include, and Why?

The first question for clarification is this: "Just what is included in each of these human resources processes?" At Hallmark we developed the model shown in Figure 8-2 to provide an overview of the components of human resources work for each of these areas. While some may organize human resources work somewhat differently than we suggest in this table, this model provided a helpful reference point for us at Hallmark. In creating it, we tried to focus on the work before we got into a design for our HR departments. But I confess that some of the groupings were done with a picture in mind of the most effective way to organize ourselves to get the work done. I think that the processes have a lot to do with structure, but I didn't want to just

Figure 8-2. The "functional technical" work of HR.

Function or Position	Workforce Planning & Staffing	Learning & Development	Organization Development	Performance Management & Rewards	Employee Relations	Diversity	Line HR Generalist
Scope of Work and Accountability	Workforce planning: • Current workforce supply (#'s and skills) • Business change drivers (e.g., strategy, work, capabilities, competencies) • Future workforce demand • Gap analysis • Staffing plans • Development plans • Transition plans Staffing: • Professional recruiting • Nonexempt recruiting • Executive recruiting • Internal staffing & placement (exempt and nonexempt) • College relations • Temporary & flexible staffing	• Employee development • Management development • Executive development • Succession planning • Career management tools & resources • Learning methodologies • Learning networks • Competency models • Competency assessment, including 360 • Competency development • New employee orientation	• Strategy development & alignment • Systems integration • Work/process design & alignment • Organization design • Change management/leadership—tools, diagnostics, leadership coaching • Environment and culture design, development, and management • Continuous improvement	• Performance objectives & measures consulting and alignment (corporation, group & individual level) • Base & variable pay programs design and administration • Executive compensation • Formal and informal recognition • Benefits program plan design, administration & communication—e.g., health, insurance, retirement, time off, education • HRIS	• Policy & practice development, application & interpretation • Complaint resolution • Issues investigation • Coaching & counseling • Performance improvement • Discipline • Employee service center • Work/life programs • Employee morale & retention monitoring • Change management • Transition management • Community relations • Health services	• Business Integration—corporate diversity strategy, priorities & plans • Affirmative action • Diversity resources & programs—e.g., ERGs, diversity circles • External presence plan—e.g., suppliers, community relations, conference & convention, multicultural marketing • Minority recruiting, development, mentoring, and retention	• Skilled at business partnership and consulting (client-aligned) • Contribute to business plans • Translate business plans to HR plans • Diagnose problems and needs • Request/broker HR services and solutions • Integrate HR services, solutions, and initiatives • Customize corporate HR programs & solutions, as required by business area • Evaluate impact of HR initiatives • Ensure client satisfaction

develop them primarily as the structure. In the end, our HR departments at Hallmark did reflect these groupings.

This model raised a variety of thoughtful questions about why we would group the work this way, including these:

- Could staffing be separated out as a unique process rather than be connected with workforce planning? Absolutely. We kept them together because we felt that the connection between planning for a needed workforce and then hiring it was critical. We wanted to make sure that those who were involved intimately in the staffing process were also intimately involved in the planning process. We felt that this would better prepare them in setting the stage for key hires. I would continue to keep them together.

- Why put succession planning as part of learning and development? Couldn't it be part of workforce planning? Once again, I believe that succession planning certainly could be grouped as part of workforce planning. After all, it is a planning process for a very specific part of the workforce. We felt that the stronger connection would be with the development process. A good succession planning process focuses significantly upon the development and preparation of executives.

- Why is the function of learning and development separate from organization development? I know that, in some companies, if you look closely at the actual work of the OD group, you see primarily leadership development. We kept these separate in large part specifically to make the point that the brand of organization development work that we wanted to create was focused on the organization as a whole—its processes and systems— and not on individuals. I believe that there is a clear connection between good organization development work and good learning and development work. My experience is that when they are grouped together, the inclination to focus on training and development tends to become so strong that these areas of work ultimately overcome the true organization development work.

- Why are "benefits" included in the performance management process? I believe that a case could be made that the benefits administration process should actually be included in a process that we did not designate that might be called "administration." If such a process were designated, I could easily see grouping benefits administration within that category. But we were also acknowledging that there is a strategic component to benefits. We felt that the benefits offered to employees are clearly part of the total reward package of the company. An employee gives the company access to his time and skills in exchange for a total reward package that includes benefits.

- "Line HR Generalists" is a grouping of work in the model. Why not instead list "Partnership" as a process? That's a valid question. I know at least one company that has decided to do just that. The reasoning is that there is a clear process for partnering with line management and connecting with the strategy, and this process is independent of the structure. I believe that reasoning makes a lot of sense.

No doubt another dozen good questions could be raised about the way this work was grouped. I never have considered this model the final answer for a static discipline but see it instead as a helpful way to think about the continually changing work of human resources.

Five Key Tasks for an HR Change Agent

In thinking about each of these areas of work, it is important to understand the tasks of an HR change agent, regardless of the particular type of human resources work. In my experience, there are five key tasks for the HR professional who will play a leadership role in a significant change effort in a business. They are these:

1. Step back from the complexity of the day-to-day environment and view the business needs through a fresh, unconstrained set of eyes.

2. Reframe the situation in a way that clarifies:
   a. What the business needs
   b. Its current reality
   c. Alternative ways to approach the gap
   d. Methodologies to transition from where the organization is today to where it needs to be tomorrow.

3. Align line leadership to sponsor the need for change.

4. Identify resources (inside and outside the organization) that will be needed in the design and implementation phases of the change.

5. Assist in the process of tracking and managing the change process.

I now explore each of these tasks in some greater detail.

1. *Step back from the complexity of the day-to-day environment and view the business needs through a fresh, unconstrained set of eyes.* This is one of the greatest opportunities and responsibilities of a truly strategic HR leader. One of the benefits of being in a staff role is the luxury of being aware of the business issues and deeply concerned for the success of the entity even while being apart just enough to comfortably step back and think—assess, analyze, and ponder. Too few business leaders take the time to do that. The strategic HR professional must take on that task. She cannot be so involved in the detailed administrative chores of tactical human resources work that she simply cannot take the mental break to pause and ponder. This step requires strong skills in systemic thinking—the ability to view the organization and the issues in holistic, connected terms. It means that she is able to see parts of a whole and make connections that others don't see.

To be effective, she needs to ask insightful and probing questions, but in a way that is unthreatening enough to allow her to garner support to engage in the changes that need making. She also must not be coerced by the current winds of politics and pressures. She must let go of preconceived notions about how the world should work. Otherwise, she will most likely stand back and see the world only as it is currently seen by those in power, those with the majority vote. Her view must be independent of coercion of any type to be of the most value to the organization.

2. *Reframe the situation in a way that clarifies current realities.* With that fresh view of the situation, one of the most important talents of the strategic HR leader is the ability to reframe what he sees. This means that he must be able to describe the current realities in ways that clarify for everyone the obstacles in the current methods for doing things and the opportunities that exist in doing things differently. In my experience, this is best done by reframing realities and opportunities visually. Most people respond well to a graphic model that helps them see complexities in a simpler way. And this provides a common language for the discussions around what needs to change and how.

3. *Align line leadership to sponsor the need for change.* As discussed in Chapter 6, a strategic human resources model absolutely requires intense and committed line management involvement. As long as a change plan is an effort done strictly by HR, it will rarely be strategic. And commitment is elusive. By that I mean that line leaders may seem committed, but it is almost impossible to predict their real reactions once the hard issues come to the front. Different leaders will pick out the portion of the initial presentation that fits their particular agendas and will disregard the elements that might later come up as challenging. It is too easy for HR leaders to breathe a premature sigh of relief when the line leader appears to have given his okay to an initiative that will be personally and politically difficult. The HR change agent should do everything possible to help the line leaders know what the hard and politically tricky aspects are likely to be and then to help them formulate their directional approach. The more this can be done before they go public with their support, the better. I discuss these political challenges in greater detail in Chapter 17.

4. *Identify resources (inside and outside the organization) that will be needed in the design and implementation phases of the change.* As in every aspect of human resources work, HR is responsible for providing the organization with all of the resources that will be needed to design and then to implement the change effort. Generally, this should be some reasonable mix of internal and external resources. Regardless of the depth of internal resources, HR must have the ability to assess what skills are needed to carry out the change effort and then to ensure their availability.

5. *Assist in the process of tracking and managing the change process.* HR plays a key role in managing the change process. This may include everything from ensuring that sponsors are adequately engaged to facilitating a group through devising a methodology to keeping individuals looking beyond the current state to the desired future state. It may include partnering with line leaders in implementation management to ensure that recommendations are carried to fruition, seeing that adjustments along the way are incorporated but do not move things off course, and ensuring that the project does not slow down too much or fail altogether.

Exploring Each Work Process

In the next five chapters, we take a good look at each of the five processes. We want to understand them conceptually, and we want to understand how they might actually be used in an organization. I explore each of these processes in terms of:

1. What this work typically involves and how it can be approached strategically

2. Frameworks we used at Hallmark to reconceptualize this work

3. Some principles and/or tools we found helpful

4. Real examples of strategic work in these areas

5. Common dilemmas or balancing acts

CHAPTER NINE

Examine Workforce Planning and Staffing Through a Strategic Lens

WORKFORCE PLANNING may be some of the most difficult and critical work in the field of human resources today, but I believe it is currently among the least advanced and least understood. It may not be glamorous work, but it is indispensable.

What Constitutes Workforce Planning and Staffing Work? What Could It Be?

Far too many companies skim over the workforce planning process if they do it at all. No aspect of human resources can be developed without having the necessary raw talent identified and brought into the organization. If talent really is the engine behind the creation of all value, identifying and bringing in the right talent is where the whole human resources process starts.

Unfortunately, even among those companies that actually have a workforce plan, too many plans are tied to—if not simply an extension of—the budget. One of the problems with linking the workforce plan in lockstep with the budget is that it assumes that the budget accurately reflects the strategy. It frequently does not. Another prob-

119

lem with this connection is that the workforce can be viewed solely as a cost item, with no way to clarify the value of people's talent as a required strategic resource. In my experience, far too few budgets offer a real reflection of a clear strategy, and the talents of people are far more than a cost. Getting the workforce plan right has significant implications for any business.

So what is a workforce plan? How is it different from a Human Resources Plan? How is it connected to the business plan? The workforce plan must be integrally connected to the strategy of the organization and the capabilities that it needs to develop to be competitive in the marketplace. If it is not tied to the strategy, it will never be of much value.

The workforce plan is a component of the HRP and the business plan that:

- Clearly identifies the number and skills of people that are needed to succeed in the business.

- Is grounded in business strategy and human resources business drivers.

- Establishes the transition plan to move from current to future workforce.

- Is an integrated part of the overall business plan.

The workforce plan itself should be broad in scope. It should encompass much more than head count numbers. It deals with these areas:

- External environment forecast
  - Industry trends
  - Demographics
  - External workforce supply and demand factors
- Internal analysis
  - Core capabilities

- ○ Pivotal roles
- ○ Broad skill set changes needed in the business
- Future workforce forecast
  - ○ By skill set
  - ○ By job
  - ○ Numbers
  - ○ Timing
- Transition plan (how we move from the current workforce to the future workforce)

This kind of examination produces a much more robust and strategic forecast than simply running some numbers.

Frameworks to Reconceptualize the Work and Some Useful Tools

In many companies, workforce planning is little more than an extension of the budgeting process and describes little more than the cost of the workforce. It often deals only with head count and misses the whole issue of transition. Managers are often measured primarily on their ability to hit a head count number. Unfortunately, there is often little value added in terms of understanding at the companywide level what skill and number changes are driven by changes in the strategy.

Workforce Planning and Transition Cycle

What is a framework for workforce planning that will allow us to more easily plan for and acquire the talent that is needed? Ann Empkey and Theresa Hupp, at Hallmark, developed the insights for the model shown in Figure 9-1 as a way to reconceptualize workforce planning process. I have adapted it slightly for my purposes here.

Part 1: Business Strategy and Core Capabilities. I am convinced that the primary obstacle to developing an effective workforce

Figure 9-1. Workforce planning and transition cycle.

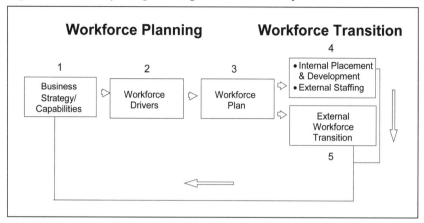

plan is the challenge of identifying with confidence the business strategy and directions for the future. This is probably the most difficult step in the workforce planning process. It pushes leaders to be clearer than they often are on their strategy and how their strategy addresses the real requirements of customers. (Chapter 7 discussed the role HR can have in helping senior leaders to examine and clarify business strategies.)

In the absence of a clear business strategy, a workforce plan is meaningless and may well create more problems than solutions. As I have emphasized already, workforce plans far too often are reactions to budget constraints and have little to do with the actual talents and skills needed to get the work done or the long-term needs of the business. Unfortunately, many managers are looking for short-term impact and are not willing to do the hard work needed to get clear on the capabilities that will enable their strategy. Getting the right workforce is one of the most strategic elements of any good business strategy. If the talent and skills aren't there, the ability to achieve the strategy and satisfy the customer won't be either.

Part 2: Workforce Drivers. With the business strategy clarified and viewed as the starting point for the workforce plan, HR and line leaders can identify the "workforce drivers." These are those implications of the strategy that will *drive* a change in the workforce. Once again, identifying the workforce drivers is hard work. It often isn't intuitive.

Workforce drivers are forces that drive significant changes in numbers and/or in the skill mix of the workforce. Examples of workforce drivers might include:

- *Technology.* Technological changes that significantly impact any work process will obviously have an effect on the required numbers and skills of a workforce.

- *Marketplace Scarcity.* When scarcity of skills is projected for certain needed areas in the business, how those skills will be acquired or retained must be carefully thought out.

- *Individual or SKU Productivity Improvement Goals.* As people or product productivity goals are established, the workforce often changes size (most frequently it is reduced). Such goals also often result in changes to work processes requiring different skills or a change in the mix of skills.

- *Work or Organization Design.* A significant redesign effort is rarely successful without careful planning for its implications for the different skills and numbers of people required.

- *Budget.* While budget is too often the primary—or only—driver of workforce changes, it is at times a legitimate workforce driver. Clearly, a significant reduction in budget will have a corresponding impact upon the workforce. When budget is a considerable driver, it is more critical than ever that cuts be tied to strategy and with attention to work redesign.

The differences among the strategy, capabilities, and workforce drivers are sometimes quite subtle and difficult to understand, and yet they are very important. Figure 9-2 illustrates how they relate to each other. Three potential strategies are used as examples, along with their corresponding needed capabilities and drivers.

Figure 9-2. Strategy, capabilities, and drivers.

Strategy	Capability	Driver
Focus on external strategic outcomes that build competitive advantage.	Ability to focus on internal ability required to fulfill strategy.	Focus on implication that drives new skills and/or head count level.
Win with new product offerings through acquisitions.	Ability to effectively acquire and integrate new businesses.	Workforce planning that requires new talent in acquisitions.
Become a low-cost provider in the marketplace.	Lowest-cost automated distribution system.	• Automation-driven workforce reduction. • New talent base required by new technology.
Achieve highest level of overall customer satisfaction.	Ability to partner with customers.	Plan to place permanent employees on-site with customers.

Line and HR leaders do themselves a great favor in learning to automatically think in terms of drivers. Once again, in my experience, this is not intuitive for many; it takes serious effort to identify the right drivers of workforce changes.

Part 3: Workforce Plan. Workforce planning should be both "top down" and "bottom up." At the highest level, data regarding workforce trends in the external environment should be given as input during a scan of the business environment prior to developing strategy. The core of the workforce planning process should occur after strategy has been determined and needed capabilities have been identified. The output of that stage is a high-level organization and workforce plan. Some division-level data feed into that high-level plan. From that high-level plan, divisions/departments generate operational workforce plans specific to their area but aligned with the original direction.

The format for the workforce plan and the level of detail included can vary. The format should meet the needs of the particular organization. What is key is that the workforce plan be designed in a way that allows tracking and managing the workforce to strategic needs. The workforce plan should become an effective tool that provides insight about the appropriateness of the current workforce against the strategic needs.

Once workforce drivers are identified, leaders need to carefully analyze the impact that the drivers will have upon the workforce requirements. They should start with understanding the changes in needed skills, knowledge, and characteristics of employees, rather than simply jump to the numbers of employees. Simply tracking "head count" is not enough.

Employee skills, knowledge, and characteristics in and of themselves are difficult to quantify. They generally need to be designed into jobs, which are far easier to quantify and track. Obviously, there are great problems inherent in using jobs as the unit to measure in a workforce plan. Some job design systems do a poor job of reflecting real skills, knowledge, and characteristics. I won't attempt to solve that issue at this point, but I believe it is a serious and challenging issue.

However, assuming that a job system reasonably reflects real skills, knowledge, and characteristics, ultimately the workforce plan itself is generally organized by jobs and job families. It then can be translated into the numbers of people in given jobs that are needed. The workforce plan should identify a baseline for how many employees are needed in a job, how much attrition is expected, and the total levels targeted within a given time frame.

Regarding the time frame, some leaders want to plan by quarters, others by years. Once again, I believe that this is entirely up to the needs of the leaders of the organization. My personal preference is to plan in terms of quarters.

The assumption should be that any number that makes it to the workforce plan is a budgeted head count. The workforce plan cannot simply be a "wish list." If the plan is not approved and supported by budget, it is not a workforce plan. Some organizations indicate the numbers of particular jobs that are desired as well as the number budgeted so that the gap is highlighted. Either way, the workforce plan ultimately needs to reflect budgeted headcount.

A sample workforce plan is presented in Figure 9-3 to show the type of information that might be included in a very basic workforce plan. In general, the plan should be kept simple or it will not be used. As you get serious about a workforce plan, you will quickly see that there are many ways to complicate a plan. Tempting as it is, try to avoid making the plan overly complex.

Clearly there are a variety of formats you can use. Again, my general note is to keep it as simple as you can. It should present answers to these questions:

- What is the nature of the workforce that we have today?
- What are the different skills, knowledge, and characteristics that we will need in the future?
- How will the numbers of employees change?
- Over what time periods?
- Do we have approvals needed to make these changes?

Make it a tool that actually tells a story. It's necessary that people be able to understand and digest it easily if it is to have the maximum influence on choices in the organization. I have seen formats

Figure 9-3. Sample workforce plan worksheet.

Organization Name:

Position Type Family/Level	Year Begin	Attrition	Net	Year End	Req'd Hires	Budget Y/N	Q1 End	Q2 End	Q3 End	Q4 End
Engineer Civil Electrical Computer	100	9	91	110	19	Y	105	107	110	110
Administration Clerks Secretaries										
Marketing										
X										
Y										
Z										
Total										

that are much more intricate and actually tell a more complete story. They are often so complex, however, that they collapse from their own weight.

Part 4: Internal Placement and Development and External Staffing. A high-level workforce plan identifies where additional talent is needed and where there is talent excess. For the talent needs, an effective staffing plan must be developed.

The staffing plan identifies the talent needed going forward and from where it will come. It may come from within the company, or it may come from outside. The more critical the talent is to the business strategy, the more attention and resources staffing should receive. There are a variety of effective staffing plan formats. I will not attempt to suggest one as the best format.

Last, this section of the framework reminds us that we need to identify a specific development plan that will develop new skills and knowledge in current employees. This will continue to be a more and more critical aspect of workforce planning as talent becomes more and more scarce. Companies will have to develop people to take on new roles. Chapter 12 examines learning and development work in greater detail.

Part 5: Transition Plan. Working on a company's transition plan is one of the most important and complicated pieces of human resources work that exists. It is a time when personal and corporate values are most strongly tested and defined. It is a time when leaders face their responsibility for choices they have made in running the business. These choices often lead to a mismatch between the supply and the demand for workforce talent. There are financial consequences to these choices. There are employee relations consequences to these choices.

When a company finds that it has employees with skills that are no longer needed, a variety of transition options might be considered. Some of them are summarized in Figure 9-4. Obviously, each of

Figure 9-4. External workforce transition.

Options for External Placement of Talent:	
Reduced Hiring	Training/Retraining
Redistribution of Work/People	Loaned-Employee Programs
Overtime	Reassignment
Technology	On-Call Pool
Shift Reduction	Job Sharing
Slow Replacement Rates	Retirement
Performance Management	Voluntary & Involuntary
Part-Time vs. Full-Time Balance Change	Turnover
Surplus	Severance
Displacement	Career Transition Assistance
Job Posting	Subsidiary Placement

these options comes with different ramifications. Some are more pleasant to the employee, and some are less pleasant to the employee. Some are more cost-efficient, and some are less cost-efficient.

Deciding whether there are still internal jobs available for current employees is always a very challenging aspect of the planning process. Many leaders subconsciously mix agendas when doing workforce planning. They intend, on the one hand, to create the most effective workforce they can. On the other hand, they are influenced to uphold real or perceived company values such as "We have a 'no layoffs' practice." In so doing, they often create significant confusion about the workforce plan's purpose. They often also ultimately develop a workforce that is less than able to deliver what is needed.

Even if the company chooses to keep all of the employees employed, it is important to keep the plan directly linked to the real needs of the business. It is far better to know the workforce that is ideally needed and to know the gaps between it and the actual workforce than to let the workforce plan become a statement of what exists instead of what is needed.

Some Principles that Guided Us at Hallmark

- Workforce planning should be both "top down" and "bottom up." As it identifies the environmental factors, it informs the strategy. But the majority of the work is driven as a result of the strategy.

- Workforce plans are driven both by:
  - Strategy and business drivers
  - Ongoing maintenance needs of the organization.

- While workforce planning is done in the context of strategy and drivers, the end result needs to be a focused statement that reflects numbers and skill mix changes in the workforce.

- Workforce planning should be done in terms of what is needed and should not be overly influenced by what the current workforce actually looks like today.

Why Workforce Planning Is Critical: An Example from DEC

In the very early 1990s, it was becoming clear that Digital Equipment Corporation was in trouble. Although it wasn't the only big hardware company that was in trouble, its troubles seemed deeper than those of its competitors. While the core problem was a complete misreading of the marketplace, part of its problem was the result of self-imposed constraints on how it managed its workforce.

After peaking in the late 1980s at 137,000 employees, DEC had slimmed down to a still hefty 125,000 by the early 1990s. At that point, a group of senior technical, economic, and HR leaders met to assess the state of the company. We realized that the marketplace was changing dramatically. The big, vertically organized players were getting beaten by smaller niche players that were far more nimble and much better able to move and adjust. Most of the big system players were vertically integrated, offering nearly everything in the technology value chain. That is how most of them had started and how most of them had become very profitable in the preceding three decades.

The problem was that all of these players had missed the changes in the marketplace. The customers were becoming far more sophisticated. They were becoming less and less dependent upon the big systems houses to do everything for them. They were looking desperately for ways to cut costs. The combination of these two forces meant that customers were able to and intent upon creating systems with hardware and software from a variety of different companies.

I recall the shock and huge debates among top management about whether a DEC salesperson could ever actually sell products from another company as part of the total package. While DEC was arguing, customers were simply beginning to require and receive just that—the best and the cheapest from whatever company would offer it.

We compared investment in product development at DEC and at its smaller niche competitors. This analysis suggested that DEC and its combined niche competitors were investing roughly the same amount in product development, but the niche players were achieving approximately 50 percent more revenues for their investment. They were also doing it with approximately half the combined population.

The group that did this analysis suggested to company leaders that DEC could not compete effectively until it was about half the size that it was at the time. This was an extremely challenging message for DEC. DEC had prided itself on never having had a layoff. While company leadership tried to be clear that this was a practice and not a policy, it was also clear that the senior leaders did not have the heart to begin down the road of a significant and drastic reduction in workforce, regardless of what the data said.

Those of us who did the initial analysis felt strongly that something drastic had to be done. We felt that DEC could not afford a slow decrease of our workforce over years. DEC didn't have years. Nonetheless, the analysis was ignored. It was ignored largely because of cultural and historical traditions of managing the workforce. People couldn't even have a reasonable conversation about drastic reduction of workforce, even though it was blatantly obvious that the corporation would go under without such a reduction.

Leaders were consumed by guilt. What could they have done differently to avoid being at this place? When should they have "leaned down" instead of "leaning up"? Unfortunately, the real needs had little to do with second-guessing who should have done what differently or even how to maintain the DEC culture. The ship was sinking, and leadership needed to look the stark realities in the eye and make hard decisions.

Instead, the reduction of workforce was gradual, and within several years the company was purchased by Compaq. It did not take long until what was left of DEC was approximately the size that was recommended in the analysis. It just got there way too slowly. Now, I don't claim that managing the workforce reductions differently alone would have saved DEC. But I do believe that it is a classic story of leaders who did not take seriously enough a workforce and business analysis that suggested the need for serious change.

This example does not make an argument in favor of or against layoffs. It makes the argument that taking seriously the workforce planning aspect of the business is critical and that this aspect can have deeply serious long-term implications if overlooked or mismanaged.

Key Problems in Workforce Planning

- Again, workforce planning is too often driven by budget. As long as workforce planning is set up primarily as a control mechanism—to control costs/head count—it will never enable strategy. Instead, it will function as a damage control function.

- Many organizations focus so much on the capabilities of the existing workforce and managing around that workforce as a given that they don't look creatively at what is possible.

- As I described earlier in this chapter, leaders who are willing to put organizational capabilities and competencies at risk to protect individual employees or who follow a "no layoffs" policy may take an ill-advised gamble. In most competitive environments, they put even more employees at risk in the long term.

- Employees are often slow to step up to new developmental opportunities. Deep down, they hope that they will be able to continue to use their current skills. They seem to believe that the problem for them will go away. Unfortunately, some companies foster this attitude by taking away the natural consequences of the failure to acquire new skills—job loss. Companies that are soft on this issue will continue to have employees who pick and choose which developmental opportunities they will pursue.

- Work redesign is too often forgotten in implementing workforce plans. For example, it is frankly too simple to assume that you can cut the number of people and do the same work in the same way with fewer people. Rarely is this successful. Too many companies have made significant cuts in a workforce only to later rehire many of the laid-off workers.

- In determining a transition plan for employees, you must balance the cost of options with the likely employee acceptance of options.

CHAPTER TEN

Examine Performance Management Through a Strategic Lens

IN ONE ORGANIZATION I KNOW, the executive compensation design and execution had become primarily finance's responsibility. The head of finance for this particular corporation had come to see executive compensation as simply another bucket of money to be managed like all of the others. If at the end of the year more money was needed, the CFO simply announced that the executive bonuses would not pay out. It had little to do with actual performance but rather reflected the state of cash flow. I often heard the rationalization for the practice described this way: "Well, at the end of the year in our homes, if the account is empty, we simply need to quit spending." While this is a nice concept for managing family budgets, it completely misses the power and role of strategic performance management and compensation.

Executive compensation programs should and can be designed with a direct connection to business results. If targets are hit, by definition the company will have plenty of money with which to pay bonuses. If they are not hit, there are no payouts needed. Simple.

Unfortunately, in this particular company, after several years when executive compensation was managed by finance as part of routine finance work, the whole system lost credibility. Many senior man-

133

agers came to be suspicious and angry about the whole process. They came to assume that their actual performance had little to do with the bonus that they would ultimately receive. While this is an extreme case, it illustrates the need for HR to bring a strategic perspective to these key people systems, a perspective that is not likely to be raised with equal effectiveness by any other functional leader.

What Constitutes Performance Management Work? What Could It Be?

Performance management is another area of strategic human resources that is in an early state of evolution. Its roots are founded in compensation. Its future, however, goes well beyond the theory and practice of current compensation and has much more to do with the overall performance of the entire entity and of groups within the entity, as well as the performance of individual employees.

In most organizations today, compensation professionals are focused almost exclusively on paying individuals competitively with the marketplace. Their primary work and personal measures focus on these areas:

- Having unimpeachable market data that make the case for what to pay a given job family. This is the foundation of traditional compensation. This gives compensation professionals the power base from which to talk about the need for certain pay structures.

- Controlling salary spending to ensure management that budgets are hit.

- Assigning jobs to a job-level structure. Many of these structures use a complex point system that is intended to give the appearance, if not the reality, of rationality. Unfortunately, these point systems are often based upon faulty assumptions about what adds value in a job. For example, do employees who run large organizations and budgets really merit the higher job levels and pay increases that these systems dictate? Not necessarily. And yet this approach often rewards breadth of responsibility far more than achieving strategic goals and meeting customer needs. Managers divert their attention from results to job leveling and are constantly fighting with HR to increase employee classification as a means to get them more money, while HR plays the bad-guy control role. This adversarial relationship is a major contributor to the broader conflict between HR and the line.

Too many compensation groups tend to focus solely on highly administrative compensation practices. In some companies, however, the function has moved toward a more strategic focus, working to influence and motivate individuals to be more aligned with the goals of the business. However, the emphasis is still on individuals. Only occasionally do HR professionals focus on team or group performance. And they rarely work on managing systems or organizationwide performance.

Unquestionably, individual performance is a key ingredient of organizational performance. However, the increased complexity, scale, and variables of organizational performance require different tools and approaches. This is a significant opportunity for HR leaders to add value to the performance of the organization.

Performance management work should be about influencing the performance of the entire entity and not just that of individuals and teams. Compensation should continue to be viewed as a critical tool in influencing performance, but as only one tool of many in influencing organizational performance.

Why Is Total Performance Management So Important?

- It aligns individual goals with organizational goals.
- It aligns individual performance with organizational performance.

- It provides insight into needed adjustments of performance and goals.

- It provides critical input for individual development planning.

Frameworks to Reconceptualize This Work

When I came to Hallmark, I found a very capable, traditional compensation group. They did the classic work of compensation well. But their thinking was not very strategic. It was not linked well to the business.

I wanted a group that did far more than traditional compensation planning and administration. I wanted to develop an HR focus that could influence the performance of the entire entity and not just that of individuals. As a key to this transition, we needed to develop some ways to think about performance management and compensation that would reframe this function more strategically.

An Evolution of Performance Management

We started by creating a visual that illustrated the evolution we wanted this group to experience: from wage and salary to compensation to performance management. This evolution is depicted in Figure 10-1,

Figure 10-1. Evolution of performance management.

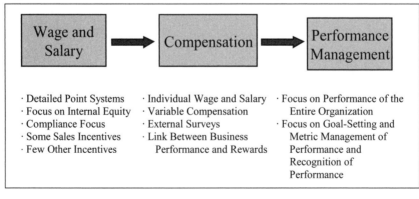

which was developed, along with the other exhibits in this chapter, by Jeff Blair, director of performance management at Hallmark. This allowed HR professionals to understand both where we'd been and where we wanted to go. First we needed them to think differently about what performance management was. Then we needed them to think about performance management from a systemic perspective.

Managing Performance of Individuals, Groups, and the Total System

With the focus on traditional compensation, little attention had been paid to the organization's overall performance or to the connection between individual and organizational performance. To help broaden the view from compensation administration to total system performance, Jeff developed a framework (depicted in Figure 10-2) that shows the relationship between corporate, group, and individual performance (down the left side) and the functions or processes of performance management (across the top). These functions or processes include:

Figure 10-2. Managing total system performance.

	Setting Expectations for Performance	Managing Performance	Recognizing Performance
Corporate	• Translate corporate vision and strategy into measurements. • Set objectives and metrics. • Communicate expectations	• Track results and provide ongoing feedback and redirection on organizational performance.	• Companywide incentives. • Executive incentives (short- and long-term).
Group	• Translate group vision, strategy into measurements. • Set objectives. • Ensure alignment and integration (management team). • Communicate expectations.	• Track results and provide ongoing feedback and redirection on group performance. • Ongoing public recognition for group performance.	• Management incentives. • Groupwide incentives.
Individual	• Mutually agreed-upon exceptions and consequences. • Development plans.	• Ongoing dialog and coaching (open, honest, and two-way). • At a minimum, midyear and formal review.	• Merit increases. • Individual incentives. • Spot awards. • Celebrations. • Praise.

- Setting expectations for performance

- Managing performance

- Recognizing performance

Where do most traditional compensation groups spend most of their time? What is their focus? Most of them focus primarily on the southeast quadrant of the framework—paying individuals. They become experts on getting people paid, efficiently and within budget.

While this is important and should be continued, it is far from enough. I didn't want a traditional compensation group that was focused solely on getting people paid. I wanted the group to focus on *why* we pay people and *what results* we are looking for as we pay people. The results question all too frequently is lost in the busy administrative tasks of getting people paid. I wanted an HR group that was as conversant about the establishment of corporate measures as it was about the current salary budget.

The total system performance framework helps line and HR understand how to integrate performance at all levels of the organization. There should not be a single employee who cannot easily see the connection between her personal objectives and those of the corporation.

Again, objectives aligned to corporate strategy are only as effective as the strategy. The strategy of the organization needs to be aligned with real customer needs. With one of my clients, it became painfully clear as we dealt with alignment of individual goals with corporate goals that almost no one had confidence in the corporate goals and strategy. When this is the case, an effective HR partner will pause the process long enough to identify the strategy gap and help the CEO or business head with a process that can fill the gap.

The total system performance framework also clarifies the need to manage and recognize performance at various levels of the organization to achieve performance expectations. Some of these approaches have a cost associated with them (e.g., create a new incentive program), and some have no cost (e.g., manage the information about performance differently). This framework offers a wide range of interventions and is useful for organizations that don't have the ability to increase financial rewards. Offering financial reward is only one of the many things that can be done to improve performance. Other aspects of motivating performance revolve around these factors:

- Clarity of the corporate, group, or individual goal-setting process
- Alignment of corporate, group, and individual goals
- Understanding of the recognition that will come for different performance levels
- Timing of performance input
- Design of recognition

Managing and incentivizing performance is not always about compensation, but, lacking an alternative mind-set about performance management work, compensation is the only lever that people pull.

Key Principles of Strategic Performance Management

Figure 10-3 illustrates the principles behind the total system performance framework. Initially, these principles may appear obvious. My experience, however, is that they are far less straightforward than might be expected.

Some Principles for Managing Performance Well

- Establish goals and metrics based on what is needed by the business strategy, not on what is possible with current skill level and practice. Too many leaders feel constrained by the current capabilities of the organization as they set goals. They do what they know they can do, rather than what they need to do to be

Figure 10-3. Performance management principles.

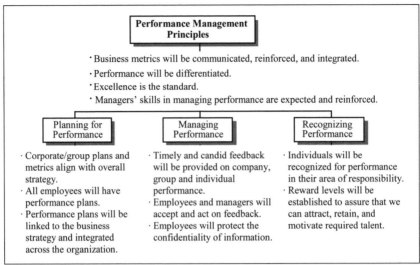

competitive. This conservative approach rarely leads to creating a strong competitive position.

- Establish clear metrics for how each goal will be measured.

- Provide honest, direct feedback. It is more helpful than sugar-coating things (more on this in the next section).

- Differentiate performance. I am amazed at how hard it is for many managers to do this. Everyone knows that we all perform at different levels, yet we seem so uncomfortable about saying so. We often design our performance systems to have a huge bias against differentiation.

- Write out goals and metrics, and make explicit agreements by both parties. This promotes clarity and defuses potential legal issues.

- Talk openly and often with employees about both performance to goals and *how* they go about accomplishing the goals.

Providing Feedback on Poor Performance

As difficult as it can be, no supervisory responsibility is more impor-tant than giving direct and honest feedback. If I have a poor performer and I continue to tell him that his performance is fine, he will have no reason to change or improve that performance. In the meantime, those with whom he will compete for future promotions or jobs are doing all in their power to develop new skills and abilities. When an opportunity comes open in two years, who will be ready? The employee whose boss gave her straight—albeit painful—input and development will be much more equipped to compete than my employee, whom I have actually set up for failure by offering only comfortable messages. I set them up because they could have been focusing on development had I been more honest in my input. And why did I choose to be "kind" and hold back honest feedback? In most cases, the truth is that I wanted the employee to feel good about me as a supervisor. I was more interested in me than in him. This misses the entire point of what real leadership is about: helping employees to leverage their skills and perform their best.

Principles for Giving Difficult Messages on Poor Performance

- Ground the conversation in agreed-to goals and metrics of measurement.
- Clearly describe actual performance against those metrics.
- Make sure that you and the employee understand the goals, metrics, and actual performance in the same way.
- Be clear about the implications of having missed a goal.
- Assess together what might have been done to achieve the desired performance.
- Identify together skill or knowledge gaps that contributed to missing the goal.
- Be clear about your expectations for this goal area in the future.

Establishing Corporate Objectives: An Example from Hallmark

A strategic HR group is one that becomes proficient in working in all nine boxes of the total system performance framework. Fortunately, the CEO at Hallmark intuitively understood the model and also had the humility to recognize that as a company we were not as integrated as the model suggested we should be. He understood that the management team did not tend to think in such integrated ways. He invited Jeff Blair, as the director of performance management, to come to the corporate executive sessions where objectives and metrics for the corporation would be established. Blair played a key role at those meetings, facilitating the executive team to establish objectives. Why was HR playing that role? Because Blair understood the need to connect the corporate objectives and metrics to group objectives and metrics and eventually to individual objectives and metrics. He also understood how to make sure that the reward systems were designed in such a way that they supported the objectives that were set.

Do I believe that HR should be leading the process for the setting of corporate objectives? No, not in the long term. We were clear that HR would play a very active role for the first several iterations of this process and then over time would slowly step out of that role. Those more logically responsible for this objective-setting function would gradually step in to play the role.

HR also teamed up with corporate communications to establish an effective system for communicating results against objectives. We had an extremely effective communications group that led a monthly conversation with the senior management team to assess actual performance against objectives and to ensure that we communicated the results effectively across the organization. This is a key part of managing performance—communicating both actual results and objectives.

Our Results

So did any of this make any difference? In my first year at Hallmark, it was clear that we were projecting to miss year-end bottom-line targets. This wasn't the first time that this had happened. In previous years, such expectations had elicited concern but led to few differences in behavior. Using the nine-box model, we determined that it was too late to redesign the rewards system that year but that we did have time to focus on the top middle box—managing corporate performance. We simply determined to communicate these items to senior managers at the end of each month:

- Their original goals
- Their current performance against those goals
- The implications of such performance for the company and its employees' profit-sharing accounts
- The implications of such performance for them personally

This was the only performance intervention made that year. It was enough, however, to ensure that year-end bottom-line goals were met.

In ensuing years, we added to this intervention of communicating differently a description of the new approach to rewards that had been designed by our line management–led performance management committee. We tied executives' bonuses much more directly to results and moved variable pay down the organization. We hit bottom-line objectives each of the next four years, as well.

Key Problems in Performance Management

Examples of problems frequently experienced by leaders include these:

- Setting corporate metrics often becomes a politically influenced event that can result in the creation of metrics with little meaning to anyone.
- Leaders typically struggle in managing the inevitable trade-offs that surface in the establishment of metrics.
- While few would go on record saying they don't want a performance-oriented culture, many act as though they don't. For example, some executives will fight a system that links reward to certain levels of performance if it interferes with their own ability

to give whatever rewards they want. In my experience, these are the very leaders who wonder why their performance is lagging. An organization that does not hold individuals accountable for performance will never be a high-performing organization.

- It can be very difficult to align individual goals with group and organizational goals.
- Engaging line managers is critical to the design and implementation of effective performance management processes, but it can be very difficult at times because of the many varied agendas that managers and HR leaders may have.
- Balancing the need to measure individual results with the need to measure group results is often challenging.
- Achieving horizontal alignment is a challenge. Even organizations that learn to align their goals vertically, from broad organizational goals down to individual goals, seem to struggle with achieving alignment across departments or businesses.

I believe that one of the hallmarks of strategic human resources is the ability to look beyond compensation and performance review formats and to engage in a system that is focused on total system performance. This is a new role for many HR professionals. Self-assessment questions might include these:

- Am I engaged as a leader in the establishment of organizational business strategies and objectives?
- Have we developed processes that align objectives at corporate, group, and individual levels?
- Do we add value in designing management processes that improve performance at each of those levels?
- Have we designed reward systems that measurably impact organizational performance?
- Are we working at a behavioral and cultural level to ensure that managers deliver honest, clear performance feedback?

CHAPTER ELEVEN

Examine Organization Development Through a Strategic Lens

I RECENTLY READ the job description for an "OD" job at a major $15 billion corporation. The focus was almost entirely on executive development and training. While this is a worthy pursuit, the description struck me as missing the core of the organization development field.

What Constitutes Organization Development Work? What Could It Be?

As I show my strategic human resources framework to various groups, more people ask for clarification on organization development than on any other area. They ask things like, "What do you consider organization development?" Or they observe, "I'm not really sure that we do 'real' organization development work."

Some think about the organization development field as dealing with a continuum of work that includes strategy development, alignment, organization and work design, continuous improvement, team development, and leadership development. Too many OD groups continue to focus primarily on the narrow slices of organizational dy-

145

namics such as training or leadership development, often missing meaty and highly influential aspects of work process and organizational design. And too often organization development efforts feel more like pet projects of the OD or HR department than design approaches that have the ability to fulfill strategy. An OD department must define organization development in a robust way that clearly links its work with the business and ultimately customer needs.

Here are some thoughts around how to envision strategic organization development work:

- OD stands for the *development* of the organization. That means, at the highest level, anything that is done to create or strengthen organization capabilities needed to fulfill the strategy.

- While things like leadership development and team building do develop the organization, these do not represent the totality of organization development work.

- The core of strategic organization development work generally focuses on the design of "organizational systems" that include environmental assessment, strategic planning, tactical planning, work flow/process design, job design and structure, corporate governance, culture, control systems, communications, and information flow systems. These systems usually cross organizational boundaries. OD practitioners must be able to look across divisions and identify how systems enable or hinder the organization winning in the marketplace.

Frameworks to Reconceptualize the Work

When I first came into Hallmark, the work of the OD group was very similar to what I described as going on in many organizations: small-group team-building exercises and leadership training. There was very little in the way of organizational systems design capability that was connected with strategy. There was some effort to help managers manage a change effort once the change had been identified, but little was being done to help the company identify the needed changes. Again, this was not robust enough for my taste.

In order for our HR group to envision organization development work differently, we found that several models were helpful to shift thinking and provide a common frame of reference. A systems perspective is the foundation of organization development work and all strategic human resources work. There are many helpful frameworks out there that illustrate this perspective.

The basic open systems star model that is often credited to Jay Galbraith for its origination has taken on a variety of forms over the years. The model in Figure 11-1 was developed by Kreig Smith, an external consultant that we used, and Eric Hansen, of Hallmark. It illustrates all of the interrelated components that an effective OD practitioner must understand and conceptualize to have a strong systems perspective.

Figure 11-2, also developed by Smith and Hansen, drills down to a deeper level of understanding by defining what each of these systems

Figure 11-1. A systems model.

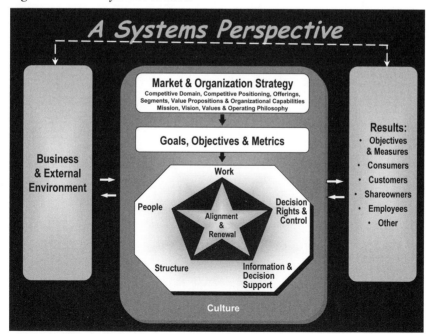

Figure 11-2. System definitions.

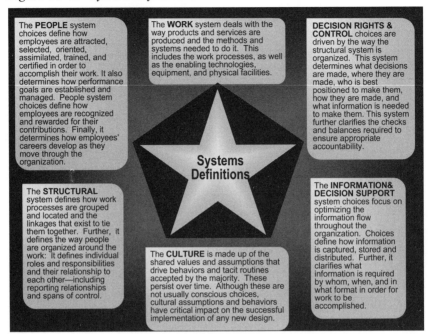

means. I found it extremely helpful in sharpening definitions of these systems and providing a common language. For example, now as we identified systems that were inhibiting the organization's ability to deliver on strategy, we had a shared language to describe these systems and an overall framework to which we attached them.

Another framework that we found very helpful in improving the quality of our organization interventions is shown in Figure 11-3, also developed by Smith and later modified by Hansen. This framework helped our OD practitioners, our HR generalists, and the rest of HR to conceptualize the different levels of organizational intervention and to understand the process for determining the appropriate level.

These are just a few of the organization development models that we used to transform organization development work at Hallmark. There are many additional frameworks that are useful in helping people understand and approach the work from a more systemic, strategic perspective.

Figure 11-3. Diagnostic framework.

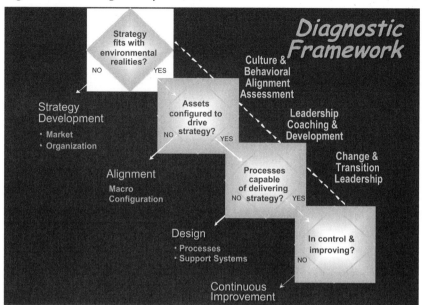

Effective OD Practitioners

Eric Hansen, the OD director at Hallmark, once categorized OD practitioners as typically falling into three camps along a continuum:

- *Theoretician*. Academic type who loves to think about the theoretical constructs and principles and ideal scenarios

- *Technician*. Give me a hammer, and I'll pound a nail. Learns one or two tools, becomes very skilled at them, and applies them to most situations

- *Technologist*. Someone who combines the best of both worlds

Theoreticians may come up with some exciting concepts and models, but unless they can take the theory and translate it into real applications, they cannot be effective practitioners. At the other extreme, practitioners who cannot understand the theoretical basis of their discipline—technicians often don't—are very limited in the number of situations where they will be effective. I believe this is the downfall of many traditional HR professionals. They learn technique without understanding the theory and principles behind what they are doing, thus limiting their scope of application.

A technologist effectively brings the two together. She knows the theory and principles of the field. She can apply these principles effectively to the specific circumstances she faces. This is the art of the field: having lots of options in terms of how to think about and approach a situation, making insightful diagnosis, and then knowing how to apply the theory in ways that make a real difference to the organization's needs.

Some Principles and Tools We Found Helpful at Hallmark

I find it particularly difficult to think over the considerable assortment of valuable organization development tools I've used in my career and narrow them down to a few principles and tools to suggest. Perhaps it is because this is my field of origin. But let me try and share a few that were particularly useful at Hallmark in transforming that OD group to engage more effectively and strategically.

Some Principles of Organization Development Work

As part of our skill development program, we outlined fundamental principles of organization development work. Some of those principles included:

- *Organizations as Open Systems.* Organizations are impacted by their environment and can adapt only when they see the "realities" (facts and accurate data) of their environment. Therefore, helping organizations and individuals identify what impacts them and see "reality" (get feedback) is critical.

- *Alignment.* There needs to be clear alignment between the:
  - Needs of the marketplace
  - Organizational strategy
  - Organization system and structural design
  - Other key human resource processes

- *Choice and Prioritization.* There are always more good things to do than resources to do them. Organization development work includes helping the organization understand its priorities and what choices follow from those priorities.

- *Clear Vision/Aspiration.* Since seeing the past is easier than seeking an ideal future, organizations tend to fixate on what has been, rather than on what can be. Organization development work includes helping the organization envision the ideal and the steps necessary to get there.

- *Formal and Informal, Rational and Irrational Components as Part of the Culture.* Culture is larger than the individual members of the organization. Organization development work includes helping members see their culture (behaviors, values, and assumptions), what drives it, and what is necessary to change it.

- *Organization Design Requires Trade-Offs and Choices.* There is no "perfect" design, only best options given the circumstances— each with an upside and a downside to manage.

Contracting is another principle and skill that is vital to all HR business partners, not solely OD practitioners. But we felt that our OD group should be particularly strong in demonstrating and instilling contracting skills. So we developed several tools around contracting, including a "contracting checklist" to review before a contracting meeting with a client. We also developed some ground rules for contracting. They included things like these:

- Contracting needs to happen at the beginning of the work/ project

- The time and energy spent contracting depends on the level and scope of the initiative—too much contracting can be as bad as too little contracting

- Direct questions and the ability to articulate your wants and needs are essential to contract effectively

- Possibly renegotiating along the way (as contracting is an ongoing process)

These principles and others guided our HR group to start thinking differently about organization development work. The systems perspective of organization development work was something we needed all our HR professionals to develop.

Design Guide

One of our challenges at Hallmark—and it's a common challenge for most companies—was that we didn't possess a lot of design skills internally, and yet those skills are crucial skills for any robust OD organization. We invested considerable effort in developing those skills (which I touch on a bit more in Chapter 16). One of the tools our OD group developed—for its own use, for HR generalists, and for any other HR professionals who want to develop their design skills—was a kind of primer on design work called the Design Guide. This tool lays out an overview and then gets into detail on the flow of a design process. Combined with hands-on experience, it can be used to teach design work to those new to it, as a reference tool for those about to facilitate design work, or as a resource for providing more detail/background to line management partners.

The Design Guide outlines a methodology that was useful for us at Hallmark; it is not rigid or static but a helpful sketch of factors to consider. The design process is divided into three phases: Getting Started, Design, and Implementation. I discuss the issues covered in the Design phase to give a sense of how the guide was structured.

Conditions for Success and Direction Setting

- How does this work fit within the organization's strategy and its value proposition?
- What is the charter of the design effort?
- How will design participants work together?

Current State Analysis

- How is work done today?
- What is working? What is not working?
- What exactly is causing variances or problems, and what are the implications?

External View

- What stakeholders will be interviewed, and which companies will we benchmark?
- How will it be done?

Visioning

- What is our expected outcome for an ideal process?
- What are the differences between the current state and our vision?

Future-State Analysis

- Design principles and criteria:
  - Among the many requirements, which are the highest priority?
  - What are the design criteria to meet the highest priority requirements?

- ○ What principles will guide design decisions?
- What will the future-state process be, and how will it work?

Support Systems Design

- What is needed to support the process in terms of:
  - ○ Structure?
  - ○ Decision making and control?
  - ○ Information flow?
  - ○ People systems?
  - ○ Culture design/change?

Process Test and Example

- How will the new process work?

- Does the design meet the value proposition, stakes, design principles, and so on established at the start of the project?

This type of overview guide increased the confidence of less experienced OD practitioners as they facilitated or assisted in a design effort. And the enthusiasm for redesigning processes to better deliver our strategy and meet customer needs spread beyond our OD group. Many of our HR generalists also used this guide to develop their understanding of and comfort with design work. A couple of our generalists were leading work flow design processes themselves, with OD consultants assisting them along the way.

Examples of Strategic Organization Development Work in Conjunction with Line Management

We did some highly strategic organization development work during my time at Hallmark. Let me give some examples. I offer them not as full-blown case studies but rather to make the following points:

- What a strategic organization development effort might look like

- What HR can do to provide leadership in such an effort

Work Redesign in Response to Marketplace Changes: The ADVANTAGE Initiative

Eric Hansen, now the OD director at Hallmark, acted as the lead consultant on the ADVANTAGE initiative. He has provided much of the description of this effort: Hallmark Cards has long been the industry leader in the greeting card business. Its focus has consistently been on providing a broad range of finely crafted, high-quality, and differentiated greeting card solutions. To create those cards, Hallmark has employed a large in-house creative staff focused primarily on the crafts of illustration and writing. Until the late 1990s, the process for product development had remained largely unchanged for decades.

Although the technological tools that could enhance the card development process had existed for several years, attempts at implementation of these tools had failed largely because the social system/ work processes had never been redesigned. Project ADVANTAGE was initiated to drive dramatic improvements in our process for designing greeting cards using digital technology to deliver:

- An *enhanced creative environment* that produces superior product and promotes digital discovery and invention to ensure sustainable product leadership

- An infrastructure that ensures a *single, sharable source* of information that is accurate, reliable, and accessible worldwide

- A *streamlined work flow* that fully leverages digital capabilities to lower total costs and optimize creative resources

Over several preceding years, the project had experienced a series of stops and starts. In each instance, the focus shifted to address different dimensions and symptoms, but one cohesive approach to address the core need and root cause issues had never been attempted. A large and cumbersome project infrastructure was in place. The initial challenge was to define new sponsorship, redefine the project scope, and reform the project's governance structure to avoid having the project implode under its own weight.

Hansen's role in this effort typified the role of HR change agent that I described in Chapter 8. As the lead OD consultant, he recognized the potential of this initiative. He could see how an improved work process would produce cards that would be more responsive to consumer preferences. He envisioned how this project in the Greetings Division could create a technological infrastructure from which the entire worldwide corporation could benefit. So he created a proposal for how ADVANTAGE could be successfully approached and completed.

Without getting into lots of detail on the actual design: Hansen did a marvelous job of creating alignment between our creative department leadership, artists, and designers, HR generalists, and the OD department to work together on this complex design effort. While HR played a highly influential role, line leaders were engaged in and led much of the process.

This design effort used a pilot approach—taking several opportunities to simulate with real product the impact of working in a distinctly different way. At the end of each pilot, results were reviewed, and qualitative input was gathered. Although it wasn't perfect, and adjustments were required over time, those who participated in the pilots gave clear feedback in support of the change. Positive feedback from the pilots began to prime the environment for change and allowed for refinement of approach before this initiative rolled out to the larger organization.

The proof points were solid, as well. Hallmark rates product at point-of-sale using an algorithm to calculate consumer appeal. Product developed using the ADVANTAGE process rated 30 percent higher at retail than product developed using a traditional process.

So what was it about this initiative that exemplified the kind of work I wanted my HR organization to do? Here are some of the differences:

- This was a high-impact change effort with significant and measurable results.

- HR was able to understand a very difficult business issue with which the business had struggled for literally a decade. HR reframed the issue in a much more holistic manner that showed the relationship among technology, work process, and culture.

- HR generalists developed the credibility needed with key line managers for them to invite HR to play a leadership role in the redesign intervention.

- OD provided world-class competence in organization system design that was able to integrate technology and work flow. OD was also able to gain the support of line management because of Hansen's fundamental understanding of the business and the manner in which he presented and facilitated the design process.

- OD and HR generalists were a seamless partnership in working with the organization.

Barriers to Growth: Organizational Business Model Design

A second example from Hallmark has to do with the evolution of the business model of the entire company. Hallmark, like many corporations, had made its name and reputation by doing several things very well: designing, manufacturing, and distributing greeting cards. Hallmark became a household name as it did a marvelous job of creating brand recognition and presence. Hallmark continues to be one of the best recognized brands in the United States. Its strengths, however, also became some of its greatest constraints. The very organizational capabilities that made it a wonderful greeting card company were getting in its way in attempts to broaden its focus into other areas.

In my first year at Hallmark, we chose to get out of the candle and picture frame businesses because we concluded that there just wasn't money to be made in those businesses. I had walked the manufacturing lines where we made candles right alongside the manufacturing lines where we made cards. It seemed to me on the surface that we were doing many of the right things in these businesses, but, sure enough, the economics just didn't work. As a new kid on the block, I assumed at the time of the decision that this was in fact a great move and didn't spend much more time thinking about it.

Over the next few years, however, the leadership team regularly visited retail in an attempt to stay in touch with the consumer and our competitors. I was struck with how often we found huge candle sections in the retail stores that we visited. They tended to have equally large picture frame sections. I was confused. I thought that these businesses weren't profitable. I was still feeling the sense of wisdom in our choice to get out of these unprofitable businesses.

As I did a bit of research, I learned that the candle and picture frame industries had actually grown significantly in the several years since we sold them. Now I was really confused. If these businesses were proving to be profitable, why had we sold them? And why did we feel certain that there was no money to be made in them? It finally dawned on me that the problem was not that there was not money to be made in candles and frames. The problem was that *we* didn't know how to make money in candles and frames. How could that be? After all, we were one of the best name brands in the world. We were a successful business with leaders who had created and managed a very profitable and successful business. What was wrong here? It occurred to me that our problem was that we were trying to manage a candle and picture frame business as though it were a greeting card business. We were using the same talent that knew cards inside and out to design, manufacture, and distribute candles and frames. We were manufacturing these products alongside cards, using many of the same people, resources, and business and manufacturing processes. The business model and processes that had been highly successful in greeting cards were exactly the wrong business model and processes for candles and picture frames.

As the HR guy, I stepped back and tried to take a strategic look at what was happening at Hallmark. I hoped to be a bit wiser than I had been in my first few months at Hallmark as we exited the candle and frame businesses. I considered the following points:

- Business growth was flat.

- We had failed at a variety of new business attempts.

- Our primary profitability strategy seemed to be continued cost reduction—a strategy that clearly had to have a point of diminishing returns. Certainly no one believed that we could really solve our fundamental problems of growth through cost management. Yet management enthusiasm for it seemed unquenchable.

It seemed clear to me that we had to develop new and different business models if we were ever to find a way to create growth in the business—business models that differentiated between the value proposition of different industries and marketplaces.

So what does the HR leader do who has diagnosed a business situation in these terms? To many, this would seem an issue that had nothing to do with HR. To me, it had everything to do with HR. We had a business problem that had, at least in part, organizational and human aspects to its root and to its solution.

My first task was to help the management team understand the concept of business models and why new business ventures were not likely to succeed using the familiar card business model that had evolved over decades. We next had to gain a broader base of management support to actually reexamine the business models of Hallmark with the likelihood of redesigning them. At this point, I felt that I had gone about as far as I knew how to go without getting additional help. I solicited the help of the company's OD director at that time, Ellen Karp, to help us better articulate the issue of business models and to identify consulting help that would certainly be needed to design this level of change. Karp and I identified several leading consulting firms and initiated high-level general conversations with them about the needs as we saw them and the current level of management support (not a lot yet) and solicited from them help in better articulating the issue to management. They were helpful indeed. They helped us to create a language with which to talk about business models.

It was a multiyear effort to transform the corporation into a business that was capable of managing discrete businesses in accordance with their specific marketplaces. Obviously, this came with tremendous challenges, some of which I discuss in Chapter 17. For the purpose of this chapter, however, I offer it as an example of the type of crucial strategic business issues that have everything to do with how a business relates externally versus internally. I offer it as an example of the kind of organization development work that HR must be able to see and lead in today's changing business environment.

Roadblocks to Progress: Corporate Culture

A third example of strategic organization development work at Hallmark was an effort to acknowledge the company's culture and its impact upon company performance and then attempt to transition the culture to be more aligned with our strategy. Corporate culture is a very tricky topic. Some say that it is far too amorphous to deal with and can't be changed. Others say that it is the core of organizational effectiveness. All I knew was that there were aspects of the Hallmark culture that had become roadblocks to progress. Everyone knew it, but had no way to legitimize the conversation, and certainly had no idea what to do about it.

I spent much of the first six months simply learning about Hallmark's business and culture. I moved boxes of cards along the printing machines. I traveled the circuit with sales professionals, trying to understand retail and wholesale. I spent time with artists. I spent time in blue jeans and T-shirt in manufacturing plants and distribution facilities doing real card production work. While this time was valuable in enabling me to learn about the product and the market, it also gave me hours to talk with people about Hallmark, its history, and how things happen there.

During the course of these months, I came to have a pretty good sense of the culture and developed a traveling presentation about the cultural observations of the new kid on the block. As is the case with most organizations, I discovered an array of cultural realities that were out of line with the culture that we wanted and needed. I began a process of conversations with groups of employees, describing my observations.

People were amazed that an officer of the company was actually willing to say publicly what everybody knew to be true. Perhaps my biggest challenge was helping some of the most senior management see the need for attention to the culture. Fortunately, the Hall family and the CEO were quick to see that there were aspects of the culture that needed to be brought back to the cultural moorings that have always been important at Hallmark. I quickly learned that strong leaders are willing to see the need for change.

As a result of this commitment from the founders—the Hall family—Hallmark was able to initiate an ongoing effort to impact the culture. HR did several key things to help leadership address these cultural issues. They included these steps:

- Get management understanding and commitment to deal with culture as a business issue.
  - Use external research
  - Undertake research with employees, customers, and vendors about Hallmark's cultural strengths and weaknesses
- Create a forum of key executives to identify the current cultural problems and the specific culture that we wanted to create. This

team determined that we wanted to create a culture that focused
on:
- The customer
- Accountability
- Performance

- Develop and implement the change plan.
  - Obtaining commitment of top management to culture change
    driven by CEO and Hall family.
  - Large-scale education of every employee about:
    - Dynamics of our marketplace
    - Financial realities of our business model
  - Redesign of key formal systems
    - Performance management
    - Executive bonuses
    - Communications of business results
  - Development and two-year follow-up by president of culture
    change plans of every corporate officer
  - Articulation of cultural dilemmas and their resolution

Why have I given you all of these examples? Organization development work is more than leadership training and team building. Some
of OD's greatest leverage is found in the design of core organizational
and management processes. These formal processes have significant
impact upon the productivity and the general feelings of employees.
HR must step into its leadership role of identifying needs for systemic
changes and then leading the organization through the complexities
and political land mines of these core changes.

Key Problems in Organization Development

When I think about the critical problems that OD professionals face
in their work, two key issues come to mind. First, managing the politics is an enormously challenging part of strategic organization devel-

opment work. Trying to put in place changes that impact the whole system, the entire organization, often means that you're messing with people's careers or power bases. There is no rulebook that can show you exactly how to navigate through those challenges. There is inherent unpredictability. In Chapter 17, I discuss this problem in greater detail and share some of my successes and failures in handling the political aspects of strategic human resources work.

The second problem that I think affects OD professionals is the risk of getting too involved in detail when you are leading designs. Many OD people get far too enthralled with process, to the point of overkill. And the level of detail in design work is often impacted by the cultural norms of involvement. Organizations with a highly participative culture are more likely to get caught up in a more tedious process.

I have been involved with process designers from time to time who bring me to my knees, pleading for a more simple way. In those instances, the problem isn't usually that the process work being proposed is without logic. I tend to find one or more of the following problems:

- The process design is being done at such a detailed level that people don't believe the assumptions that are being made.
- The process design forces people into thought processes that are inherently foreign and terribly uncomfortable because they require them to make assumptions that they would rather not have to make.

Experiences like this can leave managers highly reluctant to enter into discussions about process in the future.

OD professionals need to be very careful not to become overly infatuated in the design of process. A couple of guidelines:

- Keep the language simple and jargon-free.
- Don't feel that you have to design process down to the finest detail. Assume that people are good enough to operate at some level without an HR–driven process.

- Always connect the design of process to the achievement of results. If you can't do that, you are probably into far too much process.

Much of strategic human resources work is about influence. To influence line leaders, you must use language and a level of detail that makes sense to them.

Related to this overemphasis on process is the problem of how theoretically and methodologically pure OD professionals should insist on being about their work. I have known very bright practitioners who insist on fixing every single problem. And I frequently hear the line's perspective. which is, "I don't disagree that the problem you're identifying is real. But I don't have the time or the resources right now to address it." There are times when, as change agents, OD professionals should be tenacious about bringing an issue to the forefront. But other times, they can lose a practical perspective about trade-offs and realities in business. Organization development work is about identifying ways to improve the organization and impact the system, but timing and resources can be everything.

Experienced practitioners understand what options are available to flexibly meet the realities of available resources. There are times when it is most appropriate to walk away from a design opportunity, even when the organization design need is real. This is best judged by professionals who know what the minimum critical conditions are to achieve success.

CHAPTER TWELVE

Examine Learning and Development Through a Strategic Lens

"Hiring gifted people makes sense as a tactic but not as a strategy . . . this approach falls apart because of the scarcity of highly talented individuals."

—RAM CHARAN, STEPHEN DROTTER, AND JAMES NOEL,
THE LEADERSHIP PIPELINE: HOW TO BUILD THE
LEADERSHIP-POWERED COMPANY

What Constitutes Learning and Development Work? What Could It Be?

As I stated in Chapter 4, one of the fundamental principles of strategic human resources work is this: *Talent is the engine behind the creation of all value.* Products and services are conceived, designed, manufactured, and sold by people, through those individuals' skills, knowledge, and abilities. Talent is the source that creates value. So I don't believe that it should be difficult to draw a connection between developing talent and the fulfillment of strategy. And yet that connection is not apparent in much of the learning and development work that is done out there.

Learning and development groups seem especially susceptible to want to push the newest and most exciting piece of HR development technology. I don't know why; that is simply my experience. Many just become enthralled in the technology and the theoretical constructs. They tend to focus their work in terms of programs, courses, and tools, and too often overlook what is, in my opinion, the greatest avenue for skill development: real tasks or job assignments that stretch employees' capacities. I also see too many learning and development leaders bring in developmental activities that entertain but that may have little connection to organizational strategy or clearly assessed needs.

A Framework to Reconceptualize This Work

When I came to Hallmark, very little was being done in the way of learning and development. The primary leadership development approach was very effective internal coaching offered to individual executives by trusted HR leaders. This coaching provided a means of collecting general directions for development needs in the corporation, but there was little in terms of a systematic approach to development planning.

Figure 12-1 presents a framework that I've found useful in capturing the primary elements of learning and development. The process of learning and development is an ongoing cycle that includes the following five components:

1. *Performance Assessment.* This entire framework takes for granted that the needs of the business are captured in an effective performance assessment. And it assumes that people—starting with management—are able to honestly assess the need for development. The outcome of a development plan or program will be only as strong as is the assessment process.

   What is it that is assessed? I am a strong believer that you want to assess both *what* the employee was expected to do and *how* he did

Figure 12-1. Key components of individual learning and development.

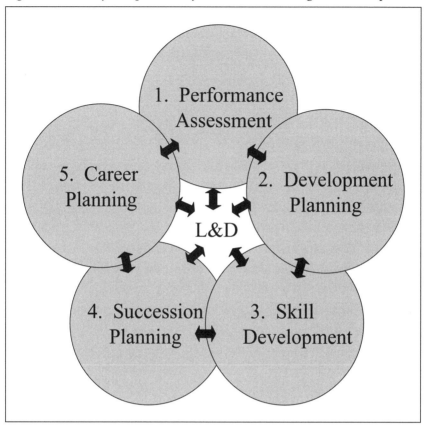

it. Generally, the *what* is best described in performance objectives. These objectives should focus clearly on results that are expected and not merely activities.

I am always amazed at how poorly most objectives and assessments against objectives are written. They tend to talk about all of the activities that were done and seem to lose sight of the results expected. Focus on the results! In addition to the results, it is also useful to assess *how* people work in terms of competencies or company values. Some of the most useful input that an employee can receive is about *how* he works, *how* he accomplishes *what* he does, *how* he tends to deal with the many subtleties that are often the real differentiators for senior-level jobs.

There are many sources of effective assessment. Clear input from the performance management process can be a valuable source of assessment if it is honestly done and focused on helping the individual perform better. Other sources of assessment include 360-degree assessment tools that gain input from boss, peers, subordinates, and, ideally, customers. Frankly, skill development is relatively easy once you really know what is needed. But, as I described, this is not always as easy as it seems.

2. *Development Planning.* The development plan should be a direct outcome of the performance and competencies review process. As a manager does a good job of assessing performance against goals and expected competencies or values, she will have tremendous input for a quality development plan. Generally, missed performance goals provide almost obvious directions for needed development.

For example, a technical leader who consistently delivers projects late may need to develop his project management skills. Perhaps another technical leader consistently delivers projects on time, but his group has the highest turnover in the company because of the intense pressure that he places upon employees to meet those goals. This may suggest the need for further development of his general people management skills.

These plans should be simple. Generally, I believe that a person can focus well on one to three developmental objectives at a time. The plan should be very clear about these points:

- What is the actual objective?

- What behaviors do you expect to observe as you accomplish this objective? Be specific. How will you know if you get there?

- Who can you sign up to help you? Let the person know specifically what you are working on and why. Find people who will be straight with you, who will give real and honest feedback on your progress.

- Identify specific things that you can do for your development. These may include job change, membership on a committee, seeking out further education, books, and articles, international work, making contacts with people from other companies, coaching, or 360-degree programs and mentoring.

Generally the development plan is directly linked to the process that assesses performance against goals (what) and against competencies (how).

3. *Skill Development.* There are many approaches available for the actual development of skills. While training plays a useful role when it is targeted at specific skills needed, other approaches that are often more successful include coaching and job rotation. These take more thought by the manager than simply enrolling someone in a training course.

And yet all one has to do is ask a group of successful leaders what were the most important developmental experiences in their careers. Rarely—if ever—will they talk about the great courses that they attended. If they do, you should be very suspicious. Most will talk about some combination of having great assignments, being part of a turnaround effort, working cross-functionally, receiving well-thought-out feedback, receiving executive coaching, mentoring, participating in international assignments, being a member of committees, being given the needed authority to get the job done, and perhaps taking an effective skills training course. Finding these kinds of development work opportunities, as I said, can take effort. And managers too often find it easier to approach developing an employee by signing her up for a course.

At Hallmark, we learned that more important than getting a technically correct development program is getting strong leadership from line management that will ensure that:

- The employee's developmental strategy is part of an effort linked directly to fulfilling the customer's needs and the business strategy

- Management clearly voices support for the developmental effort. This support is demonstrated by time and resources put into development.

4. *Succession Planning.* There are many sophisticated technologies out there around succession planning, and I will not attempt to provide that type of resource in this book. But I think it is unfortunate when HR professionals and managers, in succession planning, fail to look beyond organization charts to ask, "What is the connection between the need for succession planning and real business needs?"

At Hallmark, there were many such connections. These are some of them:

- We knew that we were moving into new business areas and would need new leaders who could take us into new arenas.

- We needed to build a leadership pool that was able to do more than cut costs, that was able to grow the business.

- We needed leadership that had an external, marketplace-focused perspective.

These and other business circumstances demanded a new look at our leadership talent and clarity on who would be leading the company in the future. I will discuss our experience with succession planning at Hallmark and some tools we found useful later in this chapter.

5. *Career Planning.* The area of career planning was not an area of work that we pursued with any depth during my time at Hallmark. I know that the philosophical questions regarding career planning are at least as important as any specific tools or programs that may be in place. These questions include:

- What role does the company have in career planning of the employee?

- What role does the employee have in career planning?

- Does the organization or the employee provide the primary direction for one's career?
- Can employees move to new jobs whenever they want to?
- What are the criteria in governing employee movement?
- How does the organization control the career movement of employees?
- What tools are available in helping in the career planning process?

Key Principles of Learning and Development

L&D leaders at Hallmark created a Development Planning Guide to accompany the Hallmark Success Profile. As part of that, they identified key principles of development, which included the following:

- Development is an *investment* in building behaviors that result in successful performance. (And, I would add, it is an investment in building capabilities that enable business strategy.)
- Most development occurs on the job, not in the classroom.
- Employees and managers are partners in the development process. Employees are responsible for their own development. Managers provide information and opportunities for employees to develop in a supportive environment.
- Competencies are descriptions of individual behaviors that define successful performance.

Succession Planning: An Example with Tools We Found Useful

At Hallmark, leaders assess senior management on the basis of performance against objectives and leadership competencies. Some companies, like GE, evaluate the leaders on performance against objectives and "potential." Potential, however, can be defined many different ways. Identifying leadership competencies may be one way to clarify a definition of potential. The Hallmark grid for its senior management group, developed by Cheryl Getty, is shown in Figure 12-2. This Leadership Assessment Matrix assesses both performance and competencies. This approach forces leaders to differentiate between performance levels and assessment of competencies. This same classification system for each individual is then used in leaders' succession management process for senior management, as shown in Figure 12-3.

At Hallmark, another essential part of succession planning is identifying key jobs in the organization. These are the positions that are the most vital for accomplishing the work of the organization. These positions also foster the development of new leaders. Identifying these key jobs enables leaders to see whether they have slow-moving people

Figure 12-2. Leadership assessment matrix.

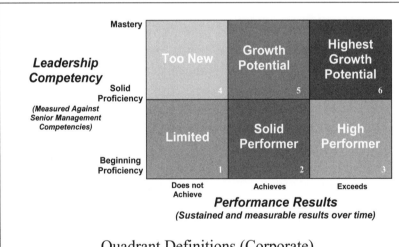

Quadrant Definitions (Corporate)

- **Highest Growth Potential**—High probability that the individual will advance into senior-level or officer position.
- **Growth Potential**—High probability of continued advancement into or within senior management.
- **High Performer**—Significant functional contribution to the organization and outstanding performance results. May handle expanded job responsibilities but has limited promotability.
- **Solid Performer**—Meets performance expectations. Solid but average performance. Limited probability of promotion.
- **Too New**—Long-term leadership potential cannot be determined due to newness to Hallmark (<12 months).
- **Limited**—Performance is unacceptable; not in control of the job at the present organizational level. Requires immediate attention. Two categories exist for this group:
   —Overstretched: Remove from current role to another function or position where skills are better matched and individual is expected to perform as a solid performer.
   —Transition from the company.

Figure 12-3. Sample leadership map.

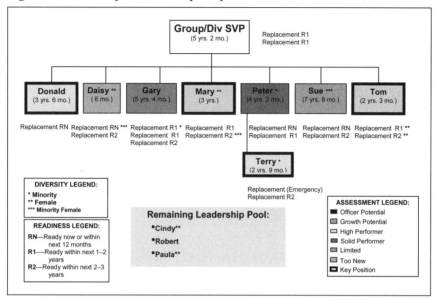

stalled in key jobs. If that is the case, a change may be necessary. They may also have strong performers stalled in key jobs. These people, too, need movement. The key to any of these approaches is that they force decisions and appropriate movement.

At times you need to go outside these traditional planning processes. After we had identified a shortlist of high-potential leaders in the company, I personally took on the task as the VP-HR to meet with potential leaders in a series of conversations about their career and developmental needs. We made it clear that it was an honor to be part of this assessment process. As a result, these leaders became very open about the need for development. They were honest about strengths and weaknesses. In addition to receiving input from the actual candidates, I also interviewed their bosses and several key people with whom they worked. My summary was then presented to the senior management group for discussion and decisions regarding their career. This was a really helpful process, as real decisions came out of every one of these reviews that placed key people into important developmental jobs.

Key Problems in Learning and Development

One of the central problems associated with learning and development work is the same as that for performance management work. Effective work in these arenas is highly dependent on accurate assessments of performance and needs, and yet accurate assessments are very elusive in practice. One reason for this is that leaders do not have the courage to recognize and share how their employees need to improve. Another is that recipients of feedback go to great lengths to avoid the pain of any unflattering self-reflection.

Daniel Goleman describes an interesting phenomenon called "CEO disease," which he says afflicts not only CEOs but also most high-level leaders. There is an information vacuum around senior leaders in general because of a widespread instinct among workers to please leaders, and this vacuum is particularly insidious when it comes to feedback on leaders' own performance. Goleman states, "Of course, many people—not just leaders—complain that they get too little useful performance feedback. But top executives typically get the least reliable information about how they are doing. For instance, an analysis of 177 separate studies that assessed more than 28,000 managers found that feedback on performance became less consistent the higher the manager's position or the more complex the manager's role."[1] Perhaps the most important area of work in the arena of learning and development focuses on developing leaders, and yet leaders are least likely to have an accurate performance assessment as their starting point.

Sometimes those below them lack the courage to tell them. And sometimes it happens because the leaders lack courage themselves. I recall one organization that agreed to sponsor an assessment effort for all managers. The intent was really to understand what the needs were so that any programmatic development design would be on target and actually be able to make a difference.

The company decided to start with top management. It used an assessment approach that had been successfully used in many companies and assumed that people were actually willing to acknowledge that they needed development. Top management was so uncomfortable with being assessed that the effort was a failure at that level. Senior managers were not open. They did all they could to cover up areas needed for development. They were extremely protective of one another in any of the exercises designed around assessment.

Unfortunately, however, they decided to continue the process with the rest of mid-level management. Although senior management didn't want to be assessed personally, they were most interested in an assessment of the next level. At the next level, employees had learned well from their bosses. They also were so culturally opposed to real assessment that the effort was sabotaged before it ever really got started. When the next level of management complained about being assessed, top management, which had not liked it itself, did nothing to enforce the need for this step in the process. In fact, top management aided in the demise of all the assessment efforts. Little wonder that top managers were never able to decide on a developmental strategy for leaders of the company, given that they never honestly assessed the needs.

Some senior managers were honest enough to say something to the effect of "What we really want is one of those nice programs that we did ten years ago. You know, a little R&R for the folks, some entertaining talks, and lots of schmoozing at nights over drinks." Many of these managers were not serious about developing leaders. They were more interested in looking good than in being good. There is a big difference. Leaders must genuinely support their own development and that of others in the organization if they are to have any real impact on the creation of value.

Note

1. Daniel Goleman, Richard Boyatzis, and Annie McKee, *Primal Leadership: Realizing the Power of Emotional Intelligence* (Boston: Harvard Business School Press, 2002), p. 93.

CHAPTER THIRTEEN

Examine Employee Relations Through a Strategic Lens

WHAT IS THE INTENT of employee relations work in an organization? The answer to this is grounded in the definition of an organization. At one level, an organization is a collection of individuals who strike a balance between their mutual individual interests and resources. Some individuals are motivated to maximize return on investments. They tend to attract others who bring highly marketable skills and talent. Other individuals are simply interested in providing baseline skills in exchange for pay. Others want to make the world, their organization, or their community a better place and exchange work for the knowledge that they are accomplishing that. Yet others seek personal and/or professional development. The work of employee relations is to strike a balance among all of these interests and offerings so that employees see mutual benefit in remaining a part of an organization.

What Constitutes Employee Relations Work? What Could It Be?

Historically, HR employee relations groups have viewed their work from various perspectives. These viewpoints include these:

- ER needs to protect the employee from management or owners.

- ER needs to protect the company from its employees.

- ER needs to teach management how to deal with employees.

- ER is an ombudsman between employees and management.

- ER manages the relationship between management and representatives of employees (unions).

No doubt there are other perspectives. Depending upon the viewpoint, employee relations work plays out very differently from company to company.

A strategic human resources perspective starts with the overall strategy of the company to determine its employee relations approach and methodology. The workforce plan, the performance management philosophy, the organizational work processes, the organizational structure, and the organizational culture also all strongly influence employees' feelings about the organization and their ongoing decisions to either stay or leave, be supportive or disruptive.

Is it all about having happy employees? Do we really buy the old adage that a happy employee is a productive employee? What about the employee who is delightfully happy specifically because he is not asked to step up to higher standards or because he is overpaid for his work? Is that the employee relations goal? I suggest that a more appropriate employee relations goal is to align the interests of employees with the organization's stated objectives of fulfilling customer needs in ways that are consistent with company values. The table in Figure 13-1 suggests some of the differences between tactical employee relations and strategic employee relations.

Questions and Principles We Used to Reframe Employee Relations Work

Hallmark has always been considered a leader in employee relations. Wherever Hallmark had a location, it was considered a great place to

Figure 13-1. Traditional and strategic employee relations.

Traditional Employee Relations	Strategic Employee Relations
• Focuses on day-to-day problem solving, often dealing with employee complaints about management and other employees. • Sees task as employee administration—assisting employees with their administrative tasks. • Provides management/employee representation. • Focuses on employee satisfaction. • Provides activities and entertainment for employees. • Manages or avoid unions.	• Focuses on development of stronger, more capable employees to meet customer and company needs. • Has a comfort level in developing employees so that they are stronger, more independent, and marketable, rather than dependent upon the organization. • Defines a more fluid, evolving relationship between employees and the entity. • Is adamant about adhering to values and agreements with employees. • Sees employees' talent as a resource of scarcity and does what is needed to develop and keep highly talent, committed employees. • Seeks effective and balanced partnership of HR with management and employees.

work. There was a very public emphasis placed on the employee. And it was not simply pretense. The Hall family feels deeply about the welfare of the employees of the company.

There is great emphasis on long-term employment at Hallmark. Turnover is extremely low by any standard. Loyalty is expected and rewarded. The employee relations culture at Hallmark, in fact, evolved to something of a paternalistic atmosphere where the company would care for the employee in exchange for loyalty.

As we tried to reexamine employee relations at Hallmark, we needed to consider carefully what we wanted to hold on to and what we needed to change. We did not use a particular model or framework to visually depict strategic employee relations. But I found that thought-provoking questions on the topic were very helpful in getting people to think differently about their employee relations philosophy and, in turn, the HR work founded in that ER philosophy.

These are some of many challenging questions that most companies should consider in determining their viewpoint on employee relations. Responses to these questions will vary; there is no one correct answer. Questions include:

- Does the company want employees to stay for an entire career? Why or why not? All employees or just those with certain skill sets?
- What does loyalty mean?
- How do we balance seniority and performance?
- Is a low termination rate good or bad?
- Do we measure results or activities?
- In general, how involved do we want employees to be in the management of the business?
- How much information can we trust to employees?

Let's briefly examine these questions.

Does the company want employees to stay for an entire career? Why or why not? All employees, or just those with certain skill sets? As I expressed in Chapter 9, leaders of a company should always be clear about the skills and talents that they will need in the future to accomplish their strategy. That is a very different objective than providing career-long employment for a particular employee base. While there are some clear advantages to having employees who want to work at your company for an entire career, management should be very cautious about defining the primary purpose of employment as career-term employment.

You want people who have talent and skills that are needed. Otherwise, the employee becomes a burden rather than a help. Once management sees the employee as a burden, there is a tremendous opening for conflict. The solution for this is always to be clear about the talent that is needed. Be planful so that you can develop and move people to the real needs. There is nothing worse than to allow employees to dictate that their current level of talent is what the company should expect and what they should expect to retain. No one wins in that scenario. Focus on getting employees ready to meet future organizational demands rather than emphasizing lifelong employment even if lifelong employment is a possibility.

What does loyalty mean? The dictionary defines *loyalty* as "n 1: the quality of being loyal; 2: feelings of allegiance; 3: the act of binding yourself (intellectually or emotionally) to a course of action." *Loyal* is defined as "adj. 1: steadfast in allegiance or duty; 2: unwavering in devotion to friend or vow or cause; 3: dependable in devotion or allegiance or affection; 'a faithful old dog.'" Management needs to think carefully about the type of loyalty that it wants to foster. Employees should think carefully about the type of loyalty that they want to offer. Loyalty in the employment sense is viewed in some companies more in terms of a loyal friend who will always be there no matter what than in terms of someone who is committed to do whatever is needed to help the company be successful. These are two very different experiences both for employer and employee.

How do we balance seniority and performance? Most companies place value of some sort on longevity of employment. This can be positive or negative. As with the first point, longevity for longevity's sake is not necessarily helpful to either the employee or the organization. Longevity that means providing needed skills during changing times is of great value and deserves to be recognized. Fostering an expectation of longevity as a commitment with few expectations that the employee will change and adapt is dangerous to both the organization and the employee. It is dangerous to the organization because it sets the stage for the worker to have an outdated set of skills, which means that the corporate strategy will be based on constraints, rather than vision. It is dangerous to employees because inevitably the day will come when the organization will need to make changes or when the employees will want to change jobs but will be constrained because they no longer have skills that are of value.

Is a low termination rate good or bad? I am always suspicious of low termination rates. This is not necessarily good news. Most organizations that take a serious look at themselves recognize that they have allowed many employees to stay on the payroll who are contributing very little. These are the employees whom no one wants to take on. These are the employees who are still allowed to lean on long-past accomplishments, often having offered very little in recent years. While many managers like to say that they have nothing but great employees, more often than not this is more a commentary on a manager who does not feel comfortable differentiating performance. Clearly the goal is not termination in and of itself. The goal is to make sure that the culture and systems in place expect high performance and do not support employment disconnected from performance.

Do we measure results or activities? One of the most challenging aspects of performance management is the tendency to measure activities, rather than results. I believe that this comes from a quirk of human nature that makes us feel uncomfortable looking a poor performer in the eye and being honest with her. Instead, we focus on all of the hard work and long hours she might have put into her job, regardless of whether they led to real accomplishment. This is not helpful to the employee or the organization. What a disservice we do to employees when we teach them over time that mediocre performance is acceptable. At some point they will want to apply for a job where the boss expects real performance results, and they will have little to show.

In general, how involved do we want employees to be in the management of the business? The answer to this question creates a completely different employee relations and general business environment. DEC was a pioneer in the design of self-managed work teams with its breakthrough work at its Enfield plant. Employees made classic management decisions regarding production scheduling and employee assignments, hiring, employee complaints, and so on. They literally ran the plant. This is a very different environment from that in organizations that focus on the individual. You will design your hiring, compensation, measurement, and communications systems completely differently, depending on which direction you lean.

How much information can we trust to employees? I am always interested in how much information that management is willing or unwilling to share with employees. The excuses for not sharing generally have to do with the competition, internal politics, or simply management's belief that employees just don't need to know. My experience is that management that errs on the side of informing employees will have an employee base that is far more productive. My experience is that employees generally want to be part of a successful business and will do whatever they can to make that happen . . . unless they are treated like children and kept away from real information.

Two Examples of Strategic Employee Relations Work

Employment Contract

Much has been written and discussed about the employment contract. (I am speaking here not about a legal contract, of course, but about the mutual expectations of employer and employee.) Unfortunately, many line managers do not seem to get engaged in these conversations. Those who will lead the successful companies of the future will have sorted out their own deeply held philosophy on such issues, and this philosophy will drive the creation of every process in their organization.

Employment contracts vary widely. Some companies have suggested that the only contract that they have with an employee is that they are offered the best development possible while the employee is with the given company. Others look to the longer term with what seems to be a more committed contract.

At Hallmark, we developed the "contract" presented in Figure 13-2, which covers several key employee relations issues. I've included this example not for the content but as an example of the clarity that company leadership should have about the relationship between the entity and the employee. This contract may not fit well for many companies.

Figure 13-2. Hallmark's employee "contract."

Values	Employees can expect:	Employees are expected to:
Individual Dignity	A workplace in which everyone is treated with honesty, respect, and sensitivity and in which each person's full participation is sought and encouraged.	Work productively with each other and treat one another with honesty, respect, and sensitivity for individual differences.
Performance	To work in a company where excellence is the standard; where meaningful work and clearly stated objectives support satisfaction of customer needs; where rewards reflect individual and business success; and job opportunities are based upon consistently high performance and the willingness to adjust to changing needs.	Work collaboratively with fellow employees to meet or exceed company standards; participate in establishing aggressive objectives necessary to support ongoing success; and contribute ideas for business improvement.
Communications	Direct, constructive, and timely feedback on individual and business performance; consistent access to the information needed to do their jobs well; and the opportunity to be heard and responded to.	Accept and act on the feedback they receive; engage in honest, constructive two-way dialogue with others; and protect the confidentiality of employee, company, and customer information.
Development	To receive information on the knowledge, skills, and abilities the business needs to achieve its objectives; the opportunity to develop to their fullest potential; and an environment that promotes learning.	Take ownership of their own careers; engage in continuous learning to improve personal productivity; and demonstrate consistently the skills needed to achieve company business goals.
Fairness	The consistent application of policies and practices with consideration of individual needs and circumstances.	Understand and apply the policies and practices of their company and work with appropriate employees to make changes to those policies as business needs evolve.

Hallmark had a fairly unique character. The last thing that leaders should do is to adopt the work of another company or consultant. They need to go through the hard work of deciding what they want their relationship with employees to be and how that relationship fits into their strategy.

Information Sharing

At Hallmark, we took a year to teach every employee in the company about the changing external environment and the realities of our internal value creation chain. We wanted employees to understand the realities of the marketplace, how it was changing, and the likely impact of those changes upon the company. Some of these changes were far from positive, which made sharing the information very challenging, given our culture, which tends to emphasize only the positive. But we wanted employees to understand the details of how the company made money and what their specific role in that process was. This has perhaps been one of the most clear cultural changes in Hallmark—its shift from keeping information very close to the management vest to engaging employees with a much more open environment.

Key Problems in Employee Relations

One of the problems frequently faced by ER professionals and managers is conflict between helping employees feel good and helping them be good. This is one of the most subtle and strategic issues in the employee relations arena. Much like parenting, in ER there is an inclination for a leader to want employees to "be happy and don't worry." This is a tremendous trap. If the primary employee relations goal is that employees feel good, we will go out of our way to shelter them from the realities of the world and their workplace. We will tend to hold back real and often critical messages about their personal performance or the performance of the organization against its competition. We will look them in the eye and tell them that they are doing just fine when in fact they are not. And why do we do that? We want them to feel good.

How do we behave differently as business leaders and/or as HR professionals if the primary objective is to help employees *be* good instead of only *feel* good? Being good is hard. Ask those who have achieved a level of excellence in their field. Without exception, you will find people who have learned to take regular and brutally honest criticism, criticism that leaves them no place to hide. They have learned to have a thick enough skin to realize that the criticism is the only way that they can ever truly be good. We often say that we want employees to *feel* good because we care about them. Much of the time, I don't believe that. I believe that too often we want to feel good ourselves as managers at employees' long-term expense. A strong employee is one who has learned that it actually feels much better to be good than to merely be told that they are good.

Another critical problem in employee relations is best described by this question: Should management feel satisfied or nervous when employees respond on satisfaction surveys that they are satisfied with the climate of the organization? Again, this is a very subtle and difficult question. We conduct employee satisfaction surveys under the apparent assumption that a "satisfied employee" is a better employee. There is at least one inherent flaw in that logic.

Most improvement—real improvement—comes from a response to dissatisfaction, not satisfaction. Most change comes because we are deeply enough dissatisfied that we stand up to change something. What is the source of satisfaction? Sometimes it is certainly the result of a sense of accomplishment from having achieved some highly challenging objective. Too often, it is a sense that life is comfortable and not exerting too much pressure. High scores on satisfaction surveys may well indicate that employees are well paid, not pushed too hard, and in comfortable circumstances. Is that what we want to feel good about? Low satisfaction scores may in fact indicate that employees are being pushed beyond their comfort zones and are stretching to *be* good.

CHAPTER FOURTEEN

Clarify the Roles of Generalist and Specialist

I HAVE ALWAYS OBSERVED an inherent tension between the roles of generalists and specialists. I have never been in an organization where this was not a serious and emotionally charged issue. The issue—from the specialist's point of view—is captured in this quotation from a talented specialist: "A generalist gave advice to line managers on my area of expertise. The information was both incomplete and incorrect. This makes the specialist look like the bad guy to the line managers . . . like we don't know what we are talking about." Another specialist said, "I feel like I never know what is going on in the business. The generalist keeps it all to herself. I don't know how to get involved in the business." Specialists don't like feeling that they are one step away from their business clients and having their work interpreted by another person (the generalist) to the organization. They want unrestricted access to line management.

From the generalist's point of view, I hear, "The specialist doesn't understand what else is going on in the organization. Specialists get involved and are so focused on their own area that they don't take time to see how it fits with other things that are going on. It really creates problems." Another generalist's perspective: "All specialists care about is their little corner of the world . . . they push their self-

186

interest and don't seem to care about the real problems of the business leaders. It makes me hesitant to bring the specialists in." Generalists may feel that the specialists lack the big picture, that they are out of touch with the reality of the business and the clients' needs and demands. They may feel caught between the client's disregard for the specialists' technical expertise and their peer relationship with that specialist.

Why There's Tension Between the Roles

HR generalists and HR specialists clash over who does what, who has most authority, and who is more important. Both roles are clearly needed, and yet the infighting between the two groups is a significant problem for many HR organizations. Even more unfortunate is the impact of this problem on HR's client groups. Employees and management are too often confused or frustrated as they get mixed messages from different people in HR. They wonder whom they should consult. In my experience, the internal users of HR resources want a simple interface with the function. Generally, they prefer to have one contact who can access any other resources that might be needed.

It has frequently amazed me that the very group that helps others resolve internal role conflicts has struggled so much with its own. Frankly, the problem often goes unaddressed, with people seemingly uncomfortable even having a conversation about the issue.

Why does this tension exist in a function that is all about people and groups working well together? It exists in HR for the same reasons that it exists in other functions. These include:

- The tension is designed into most HR organizations. We shouldn't be surprised that it exists. It is inherent in most structural designs.

- Both groups feel that they are competing for management attention and approval.

- A lack of understanding, appreciation, and trust can exist.

- The generalist role is a poorly defined and emerging role.

In addition to these reasons, normal human fears and the desire to control contribute to the problem.

Dave Ulrich has defined three different channels for the delivery of human resources work. They are:

1. Account managers

2. Centers of expertise

3. Service centers[1]

I have adjusted the titles slightly in applying these roles to Hallmark and prefer to use these titles:

1. Partner or HR generalist

2. HR specialist

3. Service center

It is helpful to understand Hallmark's HR customers, their outputs, the processes they use, and their power base, as depicted in Figure 14-1. The desired outcome is the same for every HR organization: a seamless delivery of effective human resources work that makes a difference to the organization and to employees. But looking at these role definitions, perhaps it should not be surprising that tensions exist between the roles.

Both Roles Are Vital

HR professionals often pose this question: "Which are more important—generalists or specialists?" To frame it this way is to misunder-

Figure 14-1. Hallmark's HR channels.

	HR Generalist	Specialist	Service Center
Customer	•Management & Employees.	•Management. •Generalist.	•Employees.
Output	•Interpret business strategy into HRP. •Deliver HRP.	•Expert technical HR capabilities.	•Policy and administrative processing. •Maximize quality and cost.
Process	•Partners with management. •Aligns resources. •Manages projects. •Generally distributed.	•Generally work is initiated through the generalists. •Manages projects. •Generally centralized.	•Responds to information needs. •High use of technology. •Generally centralized and/or outsourced.
Power Base	•Impact on the business. •Relationships.	•Technical competence. •Ability to deliver.	•Accuracy. •Speed. •Cost.

stand the nature of human resources. The question is not which role is more important. Better questions are "What is the nature of each of these elements of work?" "How are these roles alike, and how are they different?" "How can their work best be integrated together?" and "What does the external and internal customer really want from HR?"

Combination Roles

Smaller organizations may have only one person to act as both generalist and specialist as a result of resource limitations. In larger organizations, two distinct roles and jobs tend to emerge. Certain large organizations, however, have decided to resolve this tension by combining the two roles, though this tends to be the exception to the rule. HR professionals may act as generalists to a piece of the business and also have responsibility for a center of expertise or even a service center. Unfortunately, this is often driven by cost-management considerations and is not necessarily the best way to provide HR work. In talking with people in these combination roles, I generally find that their attention is frequently diverted to the tactical. The detailed demands of the dual role often drive out strategic work.

Profile of a Strong Generalist

When I look for effective generalists, I look for people who:

- Are strategic thinkers and systemic thinkers, with strong business savvy.
- Are full and participating members of the business leadership group.
- Participate in the development of business strategy for a given segment of the organization.
- Interpret the business strategy into a full range of human and organizational implications, providing the staff work for the HRP.
- Ensure that needed resources are available to implement the HRP.
- Sponsor specialists into the organization.
- See the HRP through to successful completion.

I look for the generalist who sits at the business table and does the strategic assessment of the needs of the organization. Her power base is in making an expert assessment, leading the effort to create an effective HR plan, and then bringing together the needed resources to implement the plan.

Bob Bloss, a tremendously effective senior-level generalist at Hallmark, commented that in selecting a generalist who will work for him, he looks carefully at how close to the business the person has been. "The key," he said, "is how quickly they can understand their business. They have to be willing to immerse themselves in the business.

After I hire someone into the generalist role, I insist that they take the first couple of months just learning the business. I know that they know HR. Otherwise I wouldn't have hired them. I need them to come to know the business. Leave all your HR skills on the shelf for the time being. Learn the business."

At Hallmark, we changed the name of the generalist role to HRO manager, or human resources and organization manager. Why did we add the "O" to the title? We wanted to emphasize the importance of understanding the broader context of HR work. Generalists should not think only at the individual level and the group or department level but always consider the strategy of the larger organization and the complex interaction of systems in the larger organization.

What Makes the Role Work?

Successful HR generalists have learned the difference between help and support. They come to know that when they "help" a manager or an employee, they do something for the person. When they "support" a manager or an employee, they help that person do something for himself. We need generalists who know how to support more and help less. Over time, an effective generalist will always build skills in her clientele, making them stronger at doing things themselves.

In order to work successfully with specialists, it is crucial that generalists relinquish their own gratification at being a technical specialist. Generalists must commit to their role and not chase after the best of both worlds. In my own career, for example, my specialization was organization development and workforce planning. As I moved into the generalist roles that I had been engaged in for the past fifteen years, it became very clear to me that I would lose the cutting-edge skills that I had had at one point as a specialist. It became apparent that the OD specialists that I had in my organization were far more capable at OD work than I was, because my focus had become that of a generalist.

Generalists must know when to let go of their specialty and when to invite others in to do that work. I remember how difficult it was in the early years to allow the OD specialist to do work that I felt quite capable of doing—that I loved doing—but I knew I had to let the specialists do their work. This was important not only for the development of the specialists but also for my development as a generalist. If I had continued to focus my attention and work on my personal specialty, I would never have had the time to truly learn the business issues required to be an effective generalist. Generalists who really struggle giving up that specialist role may need to recognize that they may be a better fit for a specialist role. Effective generalists are comfortable working through others.

Key Principles for an Effective Generalist Role

- Generalist work is a distinct competency, as described. Senior HR leaders need to take time to develop their generalists. They shouldn't assume that because a person is a top-rated specialist, he will be a great generalist. The two roles require distinctly different skills. This is not unlike the incorrect assumption that great managers come from great individual contributors.

- Generalists often come from different technical backgrounds. There is no single background that a generalist must have. However, a generalist must have strong strategic and systems thinking skills. Ideally, a generalist will have deep experience in two or more specialties.

- It is tempting to use technical skills as a power base. But generalists need to resist the temptation to act as specialists in their particular area of expertise. If they don't, it will undercut the specialist responsible for that area.

- Leveraging access to the business motivates the specialists. The generalist who learns to provide lots of access to line leaders will motivate specialists in their work.

- The broader the array of human resources disciplines (from employee relations to organization development) applied in the business, the more generalists need to rely on specialists. Generalists should err on the side of using specialists. Most generalists don't have deep enough skills in every area to provide the expertise an organization needs in every aspect of human resources.

- Effective generalists will not see program management as controlling every detail. If they trust specialists' competence, they should get out of their way and let them do their jobs. If they do not trust their competence, this is a different issue, which should be dealt with more directly.

Generalists help specialists to understand client requirements and the business issues uppermost in line managers' minds. Specialists support generalists as they think through the complexities and implications of different technical solutions.

Profile of a Strong Specialist

When I look for an effective specialist, I look for someone with the following strengths:

- Deep technical expertise
- Creativity in adapting solutions to fit clients' particular circumstances and needs
- Bias for action
- Customer service perspective—viewing one's specialty as a servant to business goals

I want specialists who are confident that their power base is their expertise—the quality of the solutions they can provide—rather than specialists who rigidly enforce and control policies in cases where it is unnecessary. Though they may not sit as often with business leaders as generalists do, that business perspective is still key as specialists create solutions that support business goals.

Specialists ideally can offer these services:

- Provide world-class, expert technologies in their given specialty arena. I use the word "technologies" deliberately—to suggest the need for a rigorous, research-based background that gives some solid reason to trust in the work that is offered. If specialists don't have world-class knowledge themselves, they need to be able to source it when needed.

- Contribute an expert functional perspective to the development of a business-driven HRP, without acting as if their specialty is more important than business needs.

- Ask themselves this question about the projects and tools they develop: "How does this support the business goals?"

- Think in holistic cross-discipline terms.

- Ensure the successful design and implementation of the HRP components for which they are responsible. They make sure that it works.

What Makes the Specialist Role Work?

The effective specialist learns the business. He becomes so familiar with the direction and needs of the business that he can propose approaches to difficult problems that prove to be exactly what is needed. Frankly, the specialist often has the role of keeping the generalist honest. At times, the generalist can become so integrated into the politics of the business that he does not see the real needs or is not willing to take risks that should be taken. A strong specialist can and should create a useful tension that ensures that the generalists are providing the best tools and processes for the businesses. This tension between the two roles can produce a very strong contribution from HR.

Just as generalists must relinquish their specialist role, it is critical that the specialists realize that their role is to be a specialist and not a generalist. I have known many specialists who have felt frustrated because they haven't felt that they have access to the business table. Clearly, effective generalists will provide specialists plenty of access to line leaders. However, the specialists must realize that it is the work of the generalists to sit on a day-to-day basis at the business table. As they do so, the generalists create relationships with the business leaders that are often envied by the specialists. These relationships are essential for the generalists to do their work.

The specialists come to understand that their power base is not necessarily in having regular consistent access to line management. Their power base is their ability to deliver world-class work that is clearly valued both by the generalists and by line management. In the final analysis, if specialists are unhappy being one step away from line management, they may be happier migrating toward generalist jobs.

It is important to realize that the work of both specialists and generalists is needed. Many specialists are just gaining experience in order to move into a generalist role. But other specialists are really passionate about their specialty, and they should perhaps focus their careers to become experts in their arena. Truly excellent specialists will always be in demand. If, on the other hand, a person wants to work on broader human resources topics, work more directly on business strategy, and be engaged more with line management, that person would probably be happier doing the work of the generalist.

Key Principles for an Effective Specialist Role

- Unpopular though it may be, the reality is that specialists are in the service of the generalists. Generalists sponsor their work among line management. Specialists need to accept this relationship. They must come to understand service as a valued arena of work.

- Power for the specialist lies in being great at what they do and being able to apply their work directly to management needs.

The more specialists prove themselves not only as technical experts but as HR professionals who grasp the bigger picture and are responsive to clients' urgency, the greater their influence and power base with both generalists and clients.

- Specialists are valued when they provide—or source—the best delivery channel available to their business. They cannot offer services inferior to those available elsewhere in the marketplace and expect to be taken seriously as business partners. Instead, when specialists recognize that internal competence is lacking, they demonstrate their value by linking clients with a better delivery source.

- Specialists coordinate their work with other specialties. While generalists coordinate the specialists' efforts at a very high level, much of the day-to-day detailed coordination must be done by specialists who understand all aspects of human resources and how each aspect influences their particular specialty.

How Generalists and Specialists Should Interface with Management

In Figure 14-2 we present the relationship among generalists, specialists, and managers. Each plays a critical role. The flow of the relationships is as follows:

1. All human resources work is initiated by a line manager who has a strategy or a need.

2. The HR generalist participates in the identification of the strategy or need.

3. The HR generalist helps in the creation of the HRP that is based upon the strategy and needs.

4. The generalist brings in needed specialists to help them understand the need.

Figure 14-2. Generalist-specialist-management interface.

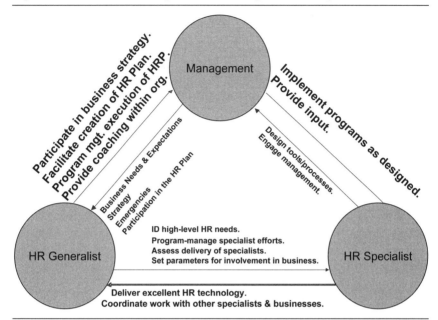

5. Specialists design required human resources processes or tools to address the business strategy or need.

6. Management plays a key role in the implementation of the human resources processes/tools.

When the Generalist-Specialist Relationship Works!

In my first job out of graduate school, I worked at DEC as an OD specialist in a new plant start-up, reporting to a bright HR generalist named Donna Blaney. As an effective generalist, she recognized the distinct contributions of the specialists and kept her ego well in check. She valued the different set of questions that I raised thanks to my organization development expertise. She did not become defensive or controlling or try to pull me out of strategic issues and focus me on tactics. She didn't need to be the organization development or strategy expert herself to be important to the organization.

Instead, she sponsored my membership on the senior management team, of which she was also a member. We spent time educating the plant manager on the advantages of having two HR people at the table. She was able to explain to him what I would bring that she couldn't. She made it very clear that when I sat at the business table with her and other senior managers, they were my clients, and I should not treat her any differently from how I treated her peers. I was overwhelmed by her insight and by her ability to leverage—rather than control—a direct report who had strengths that were different from her own. That was real leadership.

As a specialist, I certainly had to extend myself to teach her how to leverage my role. I proposed specialist work that I could directly tie to the needs of the business. I had to communicate those ideas clearly and explain how they would support business strategy. I had to demonstrate a technical competence that gave her the basis to value my work. And I certainly had to be consistent in providing quality work. She, as I described, demonstrated her intent to involve me in the key work of the organization. Through the efforts on both sides, we built a relationship of trust that made us an incredibly effective team.

Because the generalist-specialist relationship worked well, everybody won. Donna was regarded as a true leader who effectively leveraged the talent resources of the company. I won because I was able to develop relationships with senior leaders that led me to work that I would not otherwise have done. The senior leadership team won because I could see its real issues up close and design targeted solutions for them.

As I moved into more and more senior HR leadership roles, I discovered that I needed to remember the lesson I learned from Donna Blaney. This had become my model of HR leadership. As a generalist, I now needed to leverage the skills of others and not become overly controlling or need to be the specialist on every issue. I will never forget sponsoring a marvelous piece of work on organizational culture at Hallmark. This was a great piece of strategic organization development work, and I really wanted to lead that piece of work myself. Why? It sounded like fun. And it would have been great visibility, a terrific chance for a relatively new senior VP-HR to establish credibility with the senior managers in the company.

However, I had just brought in a new OD director, Ellen Karp, a very talented OD specialist whom I knew would do the culture piece better than I would. I knew that if I led it, she would lose a great opportunity to establish herself in a new organization, and it might appear that I lacked confidence in her. I reluctantly stepped aside and let Ellen lead the work. She was terrific and did a far better job than I would have. It was challenging for me to give it up, but, as a result, everybody won. The organization was impacted by a tremendous effort, Ellen's expertise was well established, and I was freed up for other strategic work that established my reputation in my new role.

So much energy and potential are wasted when generalists and specialists get distracted in turf wars. These distractions lower the value of HR in line management eyes. No one benefits. When generalists and specialists are unified in their different but complementary roles, they can turn their focus to business needs and earn the respect of their line partners.

Note

1. Dave Ulrich, *Human Resource Champions* (Boston: Harvard Business School Press, 1996), p. 112.

CHAPTER FIFTEEN

Design the Structure of Your New HR Organization

I ALWAYS SMILE when I think of how many bright leaders I have watched sit down over dinner in a dark restaurant, pull out their napkin and a pen, and start moving boxes around as their approach to organization design. It is as though they think that organization is all about boxes on the org chart. The actual structure is generally the last thing that I want to think about in transforming an HR organization. It seems to be the first thing on the mind of most managers. Too often they do this because they start by thinking about the people that they have and try to find something for all of them to do. Not a very robust theory base for structure design.

Timing and Basis of Structure Discussions

Eventually every HR leader must address the question of organization design for the HR group. I purposely postponed facing this question for the first year after I joined Hallmark because of a deep belief that organization restructuring generally should not be tackled until the work processes are defined and the desired roles are clear. I was clear that we would not act precipitously at Hallmark. I wanted to make

200

sure that we did nothing structurally with the HR group until we first understood how we wanted to approach human resources work and how we viewed the role of the HR organization in the corporation.

Basic organization design teaches this simple rule: Form follows function. In other words, structure follows purpose. Before you think seriously about how your new HR organization might look, you should first have considered the role of the VP-HR (as discussed in Chapter 5). You should also have dealt with the role of line management in doing HR work (covered in Chapter 6). You should have thought through the strategic work that you want your HR organization to accomplish (as examined in Chapters 8–13). You should also have farmed out the work to be assigned to the various other roles in the HR organization: generalists, specialists, and service center (as discussed in Chapter 14).

The following questions help assess readiness to deal with structure:

- Do we know the mission/purpose of this HR organization?
- Do we have a framework that scopes out the broad nature of the work to be done?
- Have we identified the principles that should influence the design?
- Have we determined the specifics of how that work will be accomplished? What are the processes?
- Have we determined what skills, knowledge, and attributes (or competencies) will be needed to accomplish that work?
- Are we in agreement on all of these points with top line management?
- Have we assessed the gaps between how work is done today and how it will be done tomorrow?

With all of that work done, you are now ready to think seriously about structure.

You must then consider who should facilitate the design process. Note that I did not say *lead* the process. The leadership role must remain with the top HR executive. It must be clear that she has a vision and a passion to move in a given direction. It should be clear that she can strike a balance between seeing what needs to be done and having the flexibility to allow others to play a key role in the design. One of the keys to the design work done at Hallmark was the constancy to the new vision for HR. I personally had to teach and reteach the vision and the principles at every opportunity. Until the vision is understood and accepted, design will be continually challenged and undercut.

There are a number of resources available to facilitate the design. Clearly there are excellent external resources available. You may have an internal person who is qualified and able to maintain the support and trust of members of the organization. I went with the latter approach. I was confident that the talented OD professionals I had internally could design and facilitate an effective process for us.

I wanted to make sure that the structural work was grounded in the following priorities:

- We wanted an HR organization that would help create organizational capabilities to satisfy customer needs.

- We wanted an organization that could focus on developing and delivering the corporate strategy.

- We wanted an HR structure that would be consistent with the strategic HR framework that had been developed and communicated.

- We wanted a structure that would allow HR to connect meaningfully with line management.

- We wanted a structure that would allow HR to deliver needed technical insights to the organization.

- We needed an organization that could cut costs over time.

As you work through whatever design process you choose, you should have several "check-in points" where you test whether the evolving design is remaining true to these principles.

Choosing Your Methodology

While I will not attempt in this chapter to give a robust dissertation on all of the various methodologies available for doing design, the following are some methodologies and dynamics that might be considered (please note that there are many variations of each approach that I do not detail here):

- *Back-of-the-Envelope-Over-Dinner (I have already expressed my lack of endorsement of this approach).* As I have mentioned, this is generally done when you are being driven more by placement of people than by effectiveness of work design.

- *Principle-Based.* This is an approach where a team develops a rigorous description of the principles that should drive the design. On the rigor of those principles, they then outline several generic approaches to structure and test each against the principles that have been developed. While better than the first approach I mentioned, this still lacks much of the rigor that is generally needed.

- *Work Design.* With design principles in hand, you go immediately to the process flow of work. This is an intricate and detailed process. This is often done at the detailed activity level. A careful analysis is done to identify the type of skills that would be required to accomplish that work. These skills are then grouped together into jobs. Jobs are then grouped by organizing logic, which begins to lead to a structural configuration.

These are very high-level descriptions of how you might approach an organization design.

Additional dynamics to take into consideration include:

- Who should be involved in the design process?
  - You alone? (generally not a great idea, although done frequently)
  - Small team of senior people?
  - Large group?
  - Those doing the work themselves?

- How you will finalize decisions? While I maintained final approval or "veto power," I never had to use it. We were all in agreement.

Large Conference Design

So how did we actually do the design work at Hallmark? We chose a process, called "large conference design," that would engage the majority of the HR organization in the design process. This methodology allows large numbers of people to be involved (we had approximately fifty), increasing the "buy-in" for the design, yet managing the process tightly enough to get them to make specific decisions. We chose this method because it:

- Reduced the time involved in pulling people off jobs for extended periods. (For us, the whole design was done in a very concentrated two-day period.)

- Allowed those closest to the real work to be deeply involved in the analysis and design.

- Aligned members behind a common, agreed-upon direction to accelerate implementation.

- Helped the larger community understand what was changing and why.

- Reduced the problems inherent in handoff from design teams to a larger organization.

- Got those affected excited enough to buy into changes without having been a part of the design decisions.

Judging from our goals for this process, this method seemed the best fit. Other organizations in other contexts might prefer a different design approach.

From the outset, we communicated our expectations to all the participants. We emphasized that large conference design implies:

- Open, frank, engaged debate

- Speaking from knowledge, passion, and experience rather than primarily from position or level

- Final calls that are made by the leadership team

- Decisions that are shared publicly with the full community

- The probability that needed answers are likely to be discovered in the room

These principles helped participants to think about how they could contribute and what to expect as an outcome of this process.

Reality of Cost Constraints

One of the problems we faced in this transformation is a common one for HR leaders. We needed to cut HR costs, but we wanted at the same time to add new HR offerings—more strategic business skills. I developed the model shown in Figure 15-1 to help us think about managing this dilemma. This model illustrates our expectation to lower total spending in HR by lowering the administrative-to-strategic mix of the work that we did.

I felt that it was important to be up front with the HR group about this model. I chose to talk openly about the fact that we would fund our becoming a more strategic entity by spending less on administration and tactical human resources work. We would do that by elimi-

Figure 15-1. Managing the transition to strategic HR.

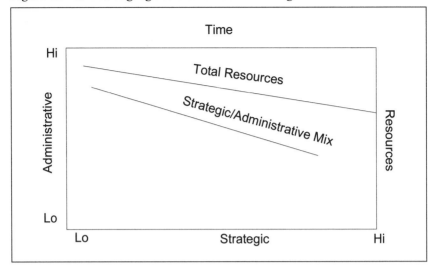

nating some work and expenditures that added little value and by doing differently the work that remained. As you might guess, this was not popular in all corners of the organization, but I felt we needed to share information about our plans and motives from the outset.

Outcome of Our Design

After our rigorous two-day large conference session, we arrived at a design that was based on the following changes, shown in Figure 15-2. We needed a structure to support the new brand of strategic human resources that we wanted to develop. We could not expect generalists to be strategic business partners and then design them into jobs that would ensure their continued involvement in the tactics of the organization.

My experience is that it is very difficult for one person to be highly effective at the tactical areas of human resources work and the strategic areas at the same time. Tactics tend to drive out strategy. At the

Figure 15-2. Structural changes at Hallmark's HR unit.

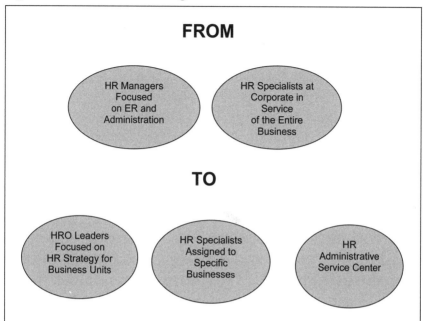

same time, we needed to structure HR in a way that enabled specialists to become more involved in the businesses, as well as to continue administration, which we did through service centers.

We would never have been able to make the required transition to a more strategic HR group without this organizational restructuring. We needed a significantly different organization to do significantly different work. The most significant changes included these:

- For the first time, we were able to have generalists (HROs) who were assigned to a business and expected to truly be the HR expert of that business. They were given extensive training (which I cover in greater detail in Chapter 16) in how to fulfill this new role. At least as important as the training, however, was the reality that they were no longer encumbered by so many administrative and employee relations responsibilities.

- We had specialists in the Centers of Excellence who were accountable to provide world-class HR technology as requested by the organization.

- We also had specialists reporting into the Centers of Excellence who were assigned to and located with specific businesses. This design element ensured responsiveness to the specific needs of the business. As time went on and deeper cost cuts were required, this group became thinner and thinner. Unfortunately, this made it far more difficult for them to stay responsive to specific business needs.

- We created a service center for the first time. Using technology, an internal administration group, and some external outsourcing, we completely changed our administrative process. This change provided significant cost cutting.

CHAPTER SIXTEEN

Assess and Upgrade Your HR Talent

WHEN I FIRST CAME TO Hallmark, it was clear that I needed to develop additional skills in the HR group. The talent base largely reflected the traditional role that the group had played for years. The staff was deeply grounded in employee relations, compensation, and benefits management. It embodied the long-established Hallmark philosophy of caring for the employee.

Hallmark had always done a remarkable job of looking out for the interests of the employee. Leaders had produced many programs that were years ahead of their time, such as profit sharing. Hallmark cut new ground by sharing profits with employees long before this was widely practiced.

HR had established a strong foundation of trust. There was no question as to whether the company cared for employees. However, this was not balanced in the HR organization with the skills and an equally strong commitment to implement a strong business strategy. HR's focus had been very administrative in nature and for the most part the department was not considered an integral part of the business discussions of the organization.

This was further evidenced by the fact that there wasn't an HR member of the senior governing body. In fact, the primary message I heard when I was interviewed for the position was about the need to add to the HR organization the ability to influence the direction and effectiveness of the business. In order to do that, I needed to create a very different talent base in HR.

There were three basic elements to my strategy for developing the HR talent at Hallmark:

1. We needed to change some key leaders.

2. We needed a series of key hires at the early and midcareer levels. I wanted to bring in new talent that had the necessary raw conceptual abilities and then give them jobs and training that would build the needed skills.

3. We needed to develop new skills among the existing talent at all levels.

Perhaps the most difficult role in any transition is the realization that the new vision for HR has raised the bar beyond some people's ability or interest to meet. In most cases, these are people who have contributed a great deal in the past, given the expectations of the time.

One of the key advantages of articulating the new vision and clarifying how it differs from current ways of working is that some people will self-select out. Some will see that the new vision is either one in which they do not want to take part or one they are not able to fulfill.

Much more difficult are the circumstances where current people really want to do the new role but don't have the skills or aptitude to do so. Now you have a difficult choice. You can choose one of these options:

• Move someone out of the new role.

• Slow down your expectations about when to fully implement the new role as the current person comes up to speed.

• Stay with the current person and possibly never really achieve the new vision.

These are the times that most define a leader's passion about the vision and test his compassion in dealing with people.

In most cases, a significant change in the vision for an HR group will require hiring some new people. This is an opportunity to bring in people who have the skills that you need to implement the new vision. At times you will find these people already in the organization, only down a level or two. This presents the opportunity to reward someone already in the organization with a promotion. Often, you need to go outside. In either case, be sure that you get the right talent, given that you are going to make a new hire.

Clarifying Your HR Competency Model

In order to develop talent, we first need to be very clear in describing the individual competencies that we need to develop. There is an interesting debate about competencies and their use in organizations. Some believe that competencies are useful only if they give you competitive advantage. This group makes the argument that since most competency models are very much alike, they obviously cannot differentiate and create competitive advantage. The group goes on to assume that little effort therefore should be spent on competency models.

I disagree. It would certainly be wonderful if competing models offered a competitive advantage in the marketplace. Competitive advantage, however, is only one of the many reasons to have a competency model. A clear articulation of desired competencies gives you a language with which to talk about your expectations for what your HR professionals should be able to do. It also gives a clear standard against which to hire and develop HR professionals.

Some HR Competency Models that I've Found Useful

There is a lot of very good work that has been done on HR competencies by a variety of groups. This research gives excellent directional insights into the skills that are needed. For example, I have once again appreciated Dave Ulrich's insights into the types of skills that HR professionals should pursue.[1] He presents four overarching competencies:

1. Business mastery

2. Human resources mastery

3. Change and process mastery

4. Personal credibility

Another insightful HR competency model was developed by members of the HR faculty at Utah State University. They relied on Dalton and Thompson's perceptive work on careers.[2] In their model, based on extensive research, Dalton and Thompson outlined four phases of career development. Although the four-stage model was originally focused on the careers of engineers, it is quite useful in other disciplines, including human resources. The advantage of this added dimension is that an HR professional can easily develop a career plan for every phase of his career. When these four phases are applied to HR competencies, they create the model shown in Figure 16-1.

In addition to the four-phase career model put into an HR context, there is another model, developed by the HR faculty at USU and presented in Figure 16-2, that allows us to think about human resources competencies in terms of skills, knowledge, and traits. This model is especially useful for its clear description of skills and knowledge—all of which can be learned and developed—as well as of traits, which may be much more difficult to develop. HR leadership may emphasize identification of these traits in the initial hiring process.

One of the major premises of this model is that skills and knowledge are not enough. We must also pay close attention to specific inherent traits in the HR professional. Skills, knowledge, and traits combine to create the needed competencies. These traits are a big part of creating personal credibility as an HR professional.

Figure 16-1. Sample HR competency behavioral indicators.

	Competencies Stages			
HR Competency Behavioral Indicator Categories	**Phase 1 Acquiring**	**Phase 2 Applying**	**Phase 3 Mastering**	**Phase 4 Influencing**
General Business Competence (e.g., Financial)	Develops a broad business and financial perspective.	Uses a broad business and financial perspective.	Increases the business and financial perspective of others.	Partners with HR council and/or SBU leadership to shape financial decisions.
Organizational Competence (e.g., Change Management)	Understands change management processes.	Diagnoses and acts on opportunities for change.	Partners with others to develop a vision for change; effectively navigates power structures.	Inspires and motivates others to sponsor cultural change.
HR Technical Competence (e.g., Compensation: Base Pay Design and Delivery)	Develops knowledge of pay design and delivery plan technical issues.	Demonstrates the ability to diagnose and solve typical design problems and is perceived as knowledgeable in the fundamentals.	Consistently develops and implements effective solutions to complex design issues; is recognized as business-focused, with a deep understanding of technical concepts and issues.	Partners with management in shaping design solutions that support benefits strategy, total reward strategy, business strategy, and corporate values.
Professional Credibility (e.g., Building Relationships of Trust)	Builds supportive team ties and relationships.	Partners with others to deliver products.	Is sought out for knowledge and mentoring abilities.	Coaches and influences leaders.

Figure 16-2. A skills-knowledge-trait model.

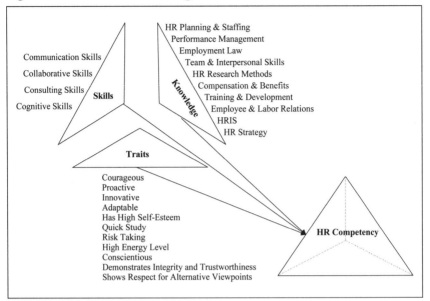

Obviously, there are many ways to think about human resources competencies. You may borrow from others' thoughts. You may create your own model. You may simply want to describe your expectations of HR professionals in your organization.

Developing an HR Competency Model

Creating your own HR competency model is not a simple task. I chose to approach it at Hallmark by talking more about expanding the existing competencies base than about starting over. I knew that I needed to do it in a way that acknowledged the good that existed in the group, yet clarified the new skills needed. Although Hallmark had remarkable competencies in a select arena of human resources work, there were many critically needed competencies that didn't exist at that point.

We created a team within the HR community to clarify the competencies that we believed were key. We wanted to use these competencies as the basis for hiring, development, and performance reviews.

Our competency model is shown in Figure 16-3. It identifies six broad categories of competencies required of HR professionals. The format of the table is the application of these competencies into a performance review form. In addition to the specific objectives that HR professionals were to accomplish over a given period of time, they were expected to build and exhibit these competencies. In the performance review process, their managers would rate them on demonstrations of the competencies. This assessment was then included in the development plan for that individual.

Assessing Priorities and Perceptions of HR Skill Levels

In my early months at Hallmark, I created the survey shown in Figure 16-4 and administered it to line management and to the HR community. Its purpose is to assess priorities around technical human resources competencies and to gauge perceptions about which competencies we did or did not have in the organization. It was fascinating to view the gap between the perceptions of the HR community and those of line management. Regardless of which competency model you decide to use, a similar assessment is very helpful and relatively easy to create and administer.

As I expected, as in most other companies, our human resources strengths were not in the strategic areas that I considered most important and necessary. This assessment was useful not only to help us understand our starting point but also to make the early case for the need to develop new skills in the HR group.

One more approach to making a very high-level assessment of your HR talent is shown in Figure 16-5. This assessment, even in its simplicity, draws a helpful connection between business needs and HR competencies. It starts by listing two to four key business strategies that your organization is pursuing. It then asks if HR is able to contribute meaningfully to these strategies in each of the human resources work areas. It is helpful to have line management do this

(text continues on page 218)

Figure 16-3. Hallmark's competency model.

HR Professional Competency/ Key Behaviors Descriptions	(Low-Med-High) Rank of Importance in Current Job	(X) Demonstrates Occasionally	(X) Knows & Applies Consistently	(X) Exemplary Knowledge & Application
Broad Human Resources Knowledge • Strong general knowledge of the human resources profession. • Broad knowledge of internal and external practices, tools, and methodologies in benefits, diversity, employment law, employee relations, HR computer systems/technology, learning & development, organization development, performance management, compensation, workforce planning, and staffing. • Applies HR processes to support successful business performance.				
Individual and Group Behavior • Firm knowledge of what influences and enables people to behave as they do, both as individuals and in groups. • Applies this knowledge in the context of integrated hr solutions. • Models this knowledge through own behavior.				
Change Management • Solid understanding of change and transition principles at individual, group, and organizational levels. • Models principles by planning, leading, and facilitating change to achieve desired business results. • Uses appropriate frameworks and tools to manage process issues. • Ensures that needs of diverse individuals and the business are incorporated into change and transition plans.				
Translating Business & Employee Needs into HR Solutions • Understands Hallmark's business and how HR processes align with and support the business. • Applies systems thinking—a holistic way of incorporating different perspectives and identifying how factors relate to each other—to translate business needs into the most appropriate integrated HR solution. • Leads strategic and tactical aspects of improving performance at individual, group, and business levels. • Delivers innovative and integrated HR solutions that make the most of Hallmark's diverse talent to achieve organizational goals.				
Building Relationships with Line Partners • Works with line partners to establish a clear definition of a performance or business problem. • Builds respect and trust, in part through forming agreements with business partners ("contracting") to ensure clarity of mutual purpose and understanding to achieve business results. • Ensures projects have clear scope, outcomes/measures, critical success factors, roles/expectations, key decisions/timing, and resources/ logistics/ budget. • Facilitates the definition of performance gaps and identifies their causes at individual, group, and organizational levels. • Draws upon an array of techniques and tools to identify and document what behaviors are required to close performance gaps.				
Enabling the Line ("Support vs. Help") • Works with business partners to achieve business tasks and to meet performance needs in a way that transfers knowledge and ownership of human resources work to line managers and employees. • Helps individual employees, groups, and organizations learn from their experiences. • Coaches others in a way that enables them past current projects and behaviors. • Supports line partners, distinguishing when helping (doing for others) and supporting (increasing the capability of others) are appropriate.				

Figure 16-4. Organization HR competencies assessment.

• **Competencies in Order of Importance**	**Level of Competencies We Have Today**
"Technical Areas" 1-9	**"Technical Areas"**
• ____Employee Relations	____Employee Relations
• ____Benefits	____Benefits
• ____(Automated) Administration	____(Automated) Administration
• ____Talent Acquisition	____Talent Acquisition
• ____Organization Development	____Organization Development
• ____Performance Management	____Performance Management
• ____Strategic Business Partnership	____Strategic Business Partnership
• ____Executive/Leadership Development	____Executive/Leadership Development
• ____Workforce Planning	____Workforce Planning
"General Areas" 1-5	**"General Areas"**
• ____Strategic Contribution	____Strategic Contribution
• ____Personal Credibility	____Personal Credibility
• ____HR Delivery	____HR Delivery
• ____Business Knowledge	____Business Knowledge
• ____HR Technology	____HR Technology

Figure 16-5. Business needs and HR competencies.

	Business Strategy 1	**Business Strategy 2**	**Business Strategy 3**	**Business Strategy 4**
Workforce Planning and Staffing				
Learning and Development				
Organization Development				
Performance Management				
Employee Relations				
Diversity				

assessment in addition to the HR community to get a sense of the differences in perception.

At Hallmark, as in many organizations, the challenge is not only to determine what your current skill levels are but also to instill a felt need for change. These assessment tools helped the HR group to recognize the need for change. And they helped HR to understand what our desired end state looked like.

Skill Development

In his HR executive recruiting, Hal Johnson has observed a lack of adequate development of future HR leaders. In my recent conversation with him, he suggested, "We still don't have enough second- and third-level HR professionals who get access to the CEO and other top-level executives . . . you know, time to put their feet up on the table and just talk about the business and its needs. And why aren't they invited? There are lots of needs. They just aren't viewed as ready to contribute. This kind of regular, contributing access will be critical to the development of the next generation of HR leadership." He pointed to companies like PepsiCo that have really gotten the development piece right and noted that HR leaders who spend time at such organizations move out to influence the whole field.

Development starts with understanding the goals—the desired skills or competencies. Once you have identified the competencies that you want to build, the difficult issue is *how* to develop them. Our strategy included the following steps:

- Teaching at every opportunity new frameworks for strategic human resources

- Teaching organizational strategy to our HR generalists and key specialists

- Putting these newly trained people in real-life situations to apply these skills

- Offering explicit training by key line management

- Requiring each HR specialty and generalist group to teach the rest of HR what he has learned

Teaching at Every Opportunity the New Framework(s) for Strategic Human Resources. We described in Chapter 4 the need for a good, sound theory base and frameworks for strategic human resources. This is crucial because, without a common and widely used framework, there is no language with which to talk about strategic human resources, what it is, how it connects with the business, and how each aspect of human resources is interconnected. The framework that we used at Hallmark is reproduced in Figure 16-6.

This framework was not simply shared one time in a kickoff meeting but was presented frequently throughout the organization, in

Figure 16-6. Strategic human resources framework.

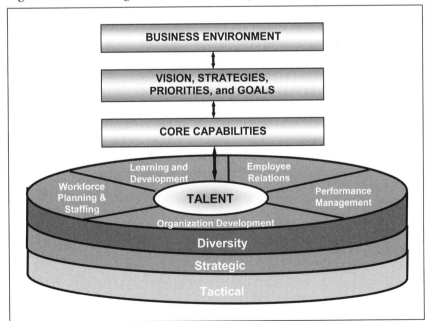

formal settings and informal settings, in large meetings and in one-on-one discussions. I tried to use it whenever I gave a presentation so that we all knew the context of the discussion. This provided HR with a common mental model and a shared vocabulary. It allowed us to stay focused on how the particular discussion should be able to enable the business. It forced us to focus on the implications of any particular effort upon other processes in human resources. I knew that the model had taken hold when it began to show up on coffee mugs, on posters in offices, and especially at the front end of HR professionals' presentations.

Teaching organizational strategy to our HR generalists and key specialists. It became very clear that while we had many bright and talented HR people at Hallmark, they had been trained over many years to think narrowly and somewhat linearly. Their contributions had been good, just not very broad or strategic. I felt that I needed to give them the skills to think and problem-solve in a much more fluid and strategic manner.

I wanted my generalists to have many of the organization development thought processes. I wanted them to be able to diagnose organizational and business needs the way a skilled OD person does. I wanted my generalists to understand organization development technologies and methodologies so that they could recognize opportunities where organizational design was needed. We named those generalist roles "HROs," with the "O" representing that organizational focus.

I contracted with Kreig Smith, an external OD consultant, and teamed him up with our OD department to design an effective program to teach organizational skills. The primary audience was the top two levels of HROs. In addition to this group, we also included a handful of key specialists who could benefit from this training. It was important that I, as the head of the HR function, be very involved in these classes. I taught several aspects of them so that the HR group clearly knew that these were not just the beliefs of an external consultant but the frameworks and beliefs of their new boss.

Components of the initial program design included these:

- Five three-day sessions were developed and conducted over twelve months. Participants in the HRO program were newly hired HROs and the HR directors who reported to me. Approximately twenty people participated in the initial program. That group went through each of the five sessions.

- The objective of the first HRO Skill Development program was to build organization diagnostic and partnering capability to enable access to line organization issues through HROs.

- The training construct was experiential and simulation-based, with pre- and postwork occurring in learning teams outside the sessions. The curriculum content was designed around the diagnostic model created by Kreig Smith and Eric Hansen, described in Chapter 11.

- Our tradition had been one of "order taking" and functional orientation. The initial challenge was to teach the new HRO partners to be certain they clearly understood the business challenges facing their particular business and not go too quickly to what was comfortable or familiar. In the future, their diagnosis would set in motion the deployment of key human resource assets in support of the businesses.

- For the new HRO role to be successful, it was critical that the incumbents develop the ability to ask root-cause questions and to understand at what appropriate level intervention was required.

The OD models previously introduced in Chapter 11 became the conceptual grounding for the development effort. We emphasized the need for and the process for:

- Developing an organizational strategy and operating philosophy
- Developing a market strategy
- Doing a stakeholder analysis
- Benchmarking
- Basing organizational design on preset criteria
- Aligning all organizational and human systems with the organizational strategy
- Aligning work with the strategy
- Designing process and structure
- Building teams

In addition to these alignment and design skills, we also felt it important to teach a broad organizational systems framework.

I wanted our HR professionals to be continually grounded in the external environment, particularly in the results that the organization sought and in the needs of the customer paying all of our salaries. Within the context of environment and organizational results, I wanted them to be able to diagnose and design systems in each aspect of the star model.

Putting these newly trained people in real-life situations to apply these skills. I was almost surprised at how quickly our OD leaders, Ellen Karp and Eric Hansen, and our senior HR generalist, Bob Bloss, came to rely on newly trained, bright young HR professionals to pick up key and very crucial aspects of important OD change efforts. They understood the need for people acquiring new skills to put them to practice immediately. They taught me an important lesson—that you have to trust that good people will step up and do what is needed. These were not efforts designed as part of the training program. These were real, "in the trenches," sometimes ugly change efforts.

Perhaps part of this trust was inspired by the fact that the new managers were desperate for helping hands. But part of it happened because they were willing to let staff try things out without needing to control everything. They did a great job of mentoring these HR early-career professionals. They spent endless hours, late nights, and weekends working with them. They taught them how to design on the fly. They taught them how to create models. They taught them how to apply and follow models. They simply had no end of time available for this batch of young HR professionals. It all paid off. Several years later, there is now a cadre of talented midcareer HR/OD leaders who are battle-tried and experienced in doing very sophisticated change work.

Explicit training about the business by key line management. I prefer to think about HR professionals as businesspeople who happen to bring a unique specialized expertise about people and organization. So I needed my HR organization to really understand the business. My assumption, however, is always that line managers are the in-depth experts on the business. I decided early that I wanted to create a connection between HR and line management.

HR professionals need to understand the business, but too many HR professionals don't sit at the business table. Too many don't have access to the strategic issues. I began a regular quarterly meeting for the entire HR group located in the corporate headquarters and for any others who could join us from out of town. A significant agenda item for each of these sessions was a lengthy presentation and conversation between a senior-level line leader (usually an officer) and the entire HR community. I wanted HR to hear about and struggle with the same issues that management was struggling with. I needed HR to learn the language of business. I invited the line leaders to engage the group. I invited them to push the HR folk to think about the human resources implications of what they were hearing.

I also encouraged the HR community to push the line leader on the business strategy being discussed. It seemed to me that there was a contingent of the HR community that became deeply engaged in these conversations over time. There also seemed to be a group that never did connect with what was being said. Some would occasionally ask why they had to sit through these presentations and what they had to do with HR. Not all HR people have the desire or ability to become strategic, and I don't, in fact, believe everyone in HR needs to be strategic. I do believe, however, that even for the most administrative of the group, there should still be a real energy about the work of the business. I wanted the whole group there. These were important opportunities to educate the HR community.

Another key help was sharing business data and budgets. HR professionals can't ask business-focused questions unless they have business data that focuses their thinking. So I began sending out the data on the business, most of which had never even been seen by HR leaders.

Requiring each HR specialty and generalist group to teach the rest of HR what he has learned. My final developmental strategy was to require that my direct reports be able to teach the rest of HR about key aspects of strategic human resources work. Between three and four years into my time at Hallmark, it was becoming clear that in most areas of our HR organization, work was being done that was highly strategic and worthy of sharing with the rest of the HR organization. As I and others attended a variety of external HR conventions and programs, we, perhaps arrogantly, came to feel that we actually had as good a story to share as many that we heard outside.

I asked each department within the HR organization to begin preparing what came to be known as its "HR Story." These stories explained how the department's work connected to the business and to the rest of HR. Managers also discussed specifically what they were doing that was strategic. They shared models and frameworks that had been developed. These stories were told to the entire HR community. They were presented at a level of quality worthy of any national HR convention. Both the preparation of and the receiving of the stories became effective methods for consolidating the learning that was going on in the day-to-day work of Hallmark's HR organization. Much is said of learning organizations. I believe that we became one as we took time to learn from our own experiences.

Keys to Success for an Internal Development Program

Kreig Smith, the consultant who worked with us on the development process, believes Hallmark was so successful in developing internal strategic HR leaders because of the following factors:

- *We clarified the expectations of strategic HR leaders.* My role was to describe exactly what I expected the HR leaders of the future to be able to do in concrete behavioral terms. Unless the target is made absolutely clear, HR professionals are not likely to hit it. When the target was clear, the responsibility for their development shifted from me to them. I also modeled those behaviors. Too often, a senior HR leader trains people in skills that he doesn't have or to which he cannot personally relate. This makes it very difficult for the professional to ever develop those skills, because the skills are not likely to be reinforced.

- *We devoted needed time and resources to development.* Hallmark devoted significant time to the development of its HR professionals. Many clients bring staff in for one to three days of training in the hope that that will "fix" them. Hallmark devoted fifteen days over twelve months to specific skill training.

- *We created real-life applications.* All who went through the program had to develop a specific organization development project

grounded in a business need. These were not contrived, but real, significant projects. They included:
- ○ Restructuring a divisional management team
- ○ Team development within manufacturing
- ○ Process redesign within the international operations
- ○ Process redesign within the creative quality organization
- ○ Coaching for the creative leadership team

- *We employed the use of internal and external resources.* We were all very clear that no one individual or company offered all the developmental help that we needed. We found that our internal people had specialties in areas that were critical. We also brought a variety of resources in from the outside that taught skills that we didn't have. In addition to drawing heavily on Smith, we brought in team development, group process, and strategy specialists to complement our skills sets. But, in the end, true HR credibility can come only from internal resources. It was the impressive work of HR and OD professionals that gained the trust of line leaders.

Development tends to be a gradual, long-term progression, and it would be simplistic to characterize it as anything but an ongoing process. However, over my time at Hallmark I observed significant changes and tremendous improvement in the HR talent. The group not only maintained its reputation as efficient administrators but earned a reputation among line leaders for bringing valuable strategic skills to the table.

Notes

1. Dave Ulrich, *Human Resource Champions* (Boston: Harvard Business School Press, 1996), p. 253.

2. Gene W. Dalton and Paul H. Thompson, *Novations: Strategies for Career Management* (Boston: Novations Group, 1993).

CHAPTER SEVENTEEN

Managing the Roadblocks in Making the Transition to Strategic HR

IF THE TRANSFORMATION of an HR organization is conceptually so clear, why is it so hard to accomplish? On the surface, it sounds like a win for everyone. Management gets a more productive, value-added organization. HR gets to be strategic and much more involved in the core of the business.

The HR change agent exists in a world of tension, living in the old world and creating the new world at the same time. He is continually working to align line managers in a way that inevitably forces them to deal with highly charged questions, some of which will push them well out of their comfort zone. He walks the tightrope of honoring the past work of the HR department and yet helping HR employees see the need to change the approaches that they have designed and learned to control. He has to push hard enough to make lots of people uncomfortable, but not so hard that they systematically reject him altogether. All of this has to be balanced with his personal sense of patience and willingness to change at others' pace. The change process is inherently full of political whirlpools that need to be carefully navigated.

Navigating the Whirlpools—Ten Learnings

From my experience with the change process at Hallmark and other organizations, I have created a list of ten potential roadblocks to making this transition in HR and developed suggestions for how to approach them. I believe that any leader transforming her HR group will face most of these realities:

1. It is hard to balance valuing the past with the need to change.

2. Some within HR will love the changes, and some will hate them.

3. The new role of HR can be threatening to some line managers.

4. Line, HR, and employees do not share a common view of human resources.

5. Some managers don't make the connection between people and business results and are unclear about the role of the HR department.

6. Many line managers are averse to examining process.

7. Diversity is not a work process but rather a subset of all aspects of human resources.

8. HR skill gaps cannot be ignored.

9. The integration of generalist, specialist, and service center roles is very difficult.

10. Communication within HR is often weak.

I make no pretense of having solutions to all of these problems. But I believe that those of us in the field of human resources often aren't open enough or don't take time enough to discuss these and other problems to have any hope of finding better solutions. By discussing some of the problems we experienced at Hallmark, I hope to contribute to the dialogue in our field to find answers to these issues.

1. *It is hard to balance valuing the past with the need to change.*
   This is one of the trickiest issues in the change process. It is

human nature to go to great lengths to make yourself and others believe that you have done exactly what was needed, that your work is exactly as it should be, that you have been marvelously successful, that you are right and the rest of the world is not. Many people are highly dependent upon the positive feedback of others. Unfortunately, as I mentioned in Chapter 10, many leaders go out of their way to give positive feedback whether it is merited or not. All of this leads to a somewhat fragile circumstance of people not wanting to go into a change effort acknowledging the weaknesses of the past. These conditions create a very complex communications challenge—to acknowledge that change is needed without destroying the morale of HR professionals in the organization.

Equally problematic is the situation where those leading the change feel a need to tear down everything about the past in order to justify their existence in leading a change. They may believe that it makes the case for change stronger, but it weakens the conditions for real change occurring. Both of these needs—to justify the past and to justify the present by tearing down the past—get in the way of effective change for the future. I have found Figure 17-1 helpful in assessing the strength of this obstacle.

Ideally, both those who are leading the change and those who have been in the organization over time will have a low need to justify either the past or justify the change by tearing down the past. Ideally, too, they will have a high desire to learn and improve. That high desire to learn and improve usually doesn't come without a sense of humility that is all too often difficult to find.

A senior HR leader at Hallmark demonstrated that rare humility with a high desire to learn. Upon my arrival, he set up a meeting to let me know that he was disappointed not to have gotten my job. Frankly, he would have preferred that I weren't there and that he were in the top HR position. He told me that his support for me would be largely based on my ability to teach him and help in his development. I told him that that was a fair request. About six

Figure 17-1. Obstacles to change.

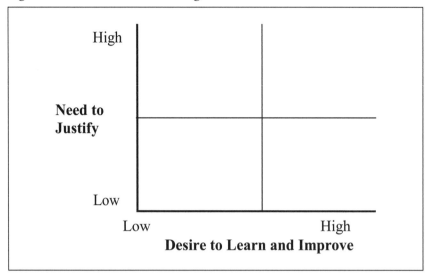

months later, he came in to tell me that he clearly was learning and was delighted that we were working together.

I had a lot to learn from some of Hallmark's current leaders. Although I recognized that my role there was to lead a change effort, I also recognized that Hallmark HR had done some remarkable work in the past and that should not be swept aside. As I mentioned in Chapter 16, Hallmark had been a pioneer in the development of profit-sharing plans. It was a leader in employee relations with a long history of strong employee loyalty. I knew it wouldn't help the change effort to have people feeling that this change was about their being failures.

So how do you acknowledge the good work that has been accomplished in the past and still create a sense of urgency around the need for change? You have to link that need to change directly to the success of the organization in the marketplace. Most likely, the circumstances of the marketplace and/or the company now require new things of HR and the company's approach to doing human resources work. That was the reality with Hallmark. My role was to help the HR organization understand that the world and its needs had changed and that those changes demanded something new, something additive from HR. Changes did not mean that people had failed in the past; they simply had been responding to a different reality.

2. *Some within HR will love the changes, and some will hate them.* It became clear that there were some in the HR department who were excited by the changes that I was proposing. They loved the clarity of the vision that HR can and should be a direct contributor to business results. That was their goal for HR as well. It was exciting to work with this group. Its members wanted to learn. They wanted to try new things. They wanted to make a difference in the business.

They were particularly pleased to see a variety of HR efforts getting the support of the CEO and top management team and that I was an active and outspoken voice at the leadership table. This was encouraging to them. This was especially the case for the early and midcareer HR professionals who were well educated and wanted to be part of a strategic HR group.

At the same time, there were clearly HR employees who seemed troubled and/or threatened by the changes. I believe that this occurred for several different reasons:

- Many in HR view the world linearly and struggle with the new systems/strategic approach used in strategic human resources.

- Some feel that their jobs and career are threatened by these changes.

- Some are uncomfortable with the different priorities of the new HR because it means their work loses priority and visibility.

Coming from a Tactical Perspective

Many in HR have been schooled for years in the administration of human resources work. As I emphasized in Chapter 1, this is clearly important work. It is work, however, that tends not to impact the strategic imperatives of the organization and that tends to be paired with a rather linear thought process in terms of how problems are approached and resolved. For this group, the conceptual frameworks and focus on strategy and systems thinking proved to be frustrating and hard to follow. It was like a new language was being spoken. In many ways, that was correct.

With this group, I didn't need or want to change them to become highly strategic in their work. I did, however, want to portray the new approach to human resources in a way that made general sense to them. Most important, I wanted to make sure that they could see how their work fit in and the importance of it. I did this through regular communications sessions with the entire HR community as well as visits with the various HR groups.

Feeling that One's Career Is Threatened

Another group that struggled with the changes included those who felt threatened by the changes. Some employees had reason to feel threatened. As I mentioned in Chapter 16, we made some changes in HR leadership in order to get the leadership and technical talent needed. These were very difficult changes and left some feeling negative about the new direction.

Others felt threatened as we introduced the concept of service centers. They could see that the company would need fewer of certain types of administrative workers over time. I chose to be very up-front about the direction we were going. I felt it important that people not be surprised. We planned to make changes to work processes that would have a real impact upon the careers of people, and I chose to let them know directionally where we were going so that they could plan for their futures. I wanted them to be able to build additional skills within human resources for the new direction of the function or to be able to look for jobs outside of HR that would fit their skills and interests.

Feeling Discomfort Over Losing Priority and Visibility

There was a third group of people who seemed concerned about the changes. These were the people whose jobs were not threatened but who had felt at the front and center of HR's agenda in the past and who struggled with sharing the podium with people who brought new and somewhat foreign skills to the party. Their arena of work was getting less attention from me and from line management than it had in the past. The issue was not that their work had become unimportant. It was very important; it just wasn't the only HR game in town anymore. This was a great challenge for some. They struggled to sort out their power base in the new HR world. I hoped to see this group step up and demonstrate a more strategic leadership approach to their functions. This happened in pockets, but not across the board.

3. *The new role of HR can feel threatening to some line managers.* This challenge is real and very difficult. In Chapter 6, I made the case for line management's involvement in creating a strategic human resources approach. Until there is real involvement of managers in creating HR's agenda, human resources work will never be adequately connected to the business. I saw three key problems arise, however, in doing this:

   - Some line managers felt that HR had forfeited its own responsibilities and was "dumping" its work onto the laps of line management.

   - Some leaders were concerned that the new design of HR systems would come at a cost to their ability to do things the way they wanted.

   - As HR became more and more involved in truly strategic issues, it drew attention to increasingly sensitive political questions. These often had significant power and structural implications. Some line managers who felt personally impacted by the potential or reality of these changes saw HR as the cause of their problems. And sometimes they would pressure HR in ways that they never would have used with other line managers.

Some of these challenges just come with the territory. But there are some things that can mitigate these reactions. It is especially important that HR people stay very involved with line managers as they engage in human resources work. This allows HR to sense how line managers are feeling about their role and respond as needed.

Suspicion that HR Is Forfeiting Its Responsibilities

There is a fine balance between line managers doing appropriate human resources work and, in fact, their having HR's work dumped on them. As I describe in Chapter 6, the first time I proposed that the line play the lead role in establishing the HR Plan for the corporation, line leaders were for the most part delighted. A manager who was going to lead the group developing the direction for performance management said, almost in amazement, "You mean that I will be able to set the direction for compensation for the company?" His experience with HR on compensation issues had always been that HR and its systems controlled him and seemed to block him at every point in doing what he wanted to do. Now he actually had control. He was like a kid in the candy shop.

The candy shop proved to be too exciting for this particular leader and his group. They started meeting at least monthly, sometimes weekly, rather than quarterly, as we'd expected. Their task originally was to set the highest-level direction and strategy, not to get down into the design of new human resources systems as they were doing. That was the HR experts' job. But we loved their enthusiasm and were quick to give them more and more rope. Unfortunately, the more involved they became, the more they felt that they were doing HR's job. They were probably right. Ironically, this same leader was the only leader to later express concern that HR was dumping its responsibility on management.

I think the learning here is clear. We should continue to bring managers into the human resources planning process. This is critical.

However, keep them at the high and strategic level. Don't let them come down and work in the details.

Concern that Autonomy Over Human Resources Systems Will Be Threatened

The second issue I mentioned is that some line leaders are concerned that the design of human resources systems comes at a cost to their autonomy to do things the way they want. For example, at one company we redesigned the executive compensation system with the intention of holding the top of the house accountable for results. The new system clarified specific results and outlined specific rewards that would come upon their achievement. To the amazement of many, the bottom-line results began to show significant improvement—almost immediately. To the excitement of senior managers, the promised rewards were paid out. As a result, this system received strong support from the board of directors and the senior management team. Many felt that there was a direct connection between this compensation change and the improved performance.

The problem came in the first year that performance was not achieved after about four or five strong years. Now the senior management team and the board had a dilemma. How would they pay the executives after they had missed their goals? For some of them, it became an overwhelming problem. They couldn't imagine not giving out traditionally high bonus payouts. It became such a problem that they chose to reduce the next year's goals so that strong payouts would occur.

There are many and often competing agendas held by executive leadership. Balancing them is very difficult. I felt that the first year of poor performance was actually a great opportunity to make the case to management that this system was real. Performance really did make a difference. What I had missed is that for some leaders, while performance was important, it was not the only agenda with which they were involved.

What did I learn from this experience? HR leadership needs to always be clear about the real motivations behind the design of certain human resources systems. Don't be deceived that it is primarily about simple principles of performance and excellence. There are many who are driven by other purposes, and it's important to uncover those motivations as early as possible and deal with them in your design process.

Opposition Because Power Is Threatened

This one is perhaps the most difficult. HR often raises sensitive questions regarding strategy and the structures required to implement the strategy. This is exactly what a good HR leader should do—any HR leader who is not raising questions that create discomfort among management is probably not raising the right or core questions. But the balance here is incredibly challenging.

Anytime that a human resources effort impacts the fundamental power structure of the organization, the political scenario will become very complex and difficult to manage. HR will likely be viewed as the source of the change and therefore a threat. Be prepared to become the target of tremendous pressure. Be prepared also to see the design that made perfect sense on paper be adjusted and changed for political expediency once the changes become more real.

I mention this to raise the point that HR will elevate issues that are highly charged with political nuances—a direct assault on the establishment—if it is doing its strategic job. In so doing, it needs to be keenly aware of the reactions and deep pressures that can be unleashed in response. I cannot give a standard answer on how to resolve this for every company because the politics and power issues are different in each. But it is a serious challenge that HR leaders should understand and anticipate.

4. *Line, HR, and employees do not share a common view of human resources.* I have brought a strong set of beliefs and assumptions

about people and the role of human resources in organizations to each job that I have had. Others do, too. Whether these beliefs and assumptions are clearly articulated or intuitive and organic, they are generally strongly held. This is one of the reasons that I strongly support the need to develop a common language and approach to human resources. Without a common language, it is hard to even have productive discussions.

I have had the opportunity to work with and for many line and HR leaders who represent a wide array to views about human resources. My first line boss was Bel Cross. He was the plant manager for a new plant start-up in Augusta, Maine. He was a young, bright, and aggressive leader with a refreshing intuition about strategic human resources. He just needed someone to translate that intuition into action. He let me become part of the leadership team with the expectation that I could then learn firsthand what needed to change.

I worked for another line leader of a major company who sat me down one day and said in effect, "I know that you really do believe the people values that you espouse. I also know that many executives say that they agree with them as well. Let me just be straight. No one cares about people. They and I are only interested in the bottom-line results of the business. Don't ever believe that we care about anything else." While I appreciated his frankness, I was dismayed by the stark contrast that I felt between his and my own views on human resources.

My point is simply that we need to stay aware of the vast and differing views held about human resources. We're too often unaware of assumptions we're making that others see things just as we see them. We need to take time to ask more questions and listen to others' views, definitions, assumptions, and expectations about human resources so that we know how to start working with them. We need to express our views of human resources in language that makes sense to them.

5. *Some managers don't make the connection between people and business results and are unclear about the role of the HR department.*

While I think that this is becoming a less pronounced issue, I have worked with a surprising number of line managers who behave as though business and its results were entirely disconnected from people and the HR department. They tend to see the HR department as dealing solely with the administrative aspects of people support, a kind of necessary evil that management has to tolerate. These managers tend to be consumed with their domain of expertise, whether that be technology, product development, finance, manufacturing, or marketing. They view the world through domain/technical eyes. They seem to miss the connection that it is only people who can further the work of the domain.

As a result, such managers tend to want HR to handle all of the "people-related stuff" so that they can get on with the important work of their domain. They want HR to hire, to manage performance, and to fire if needed. In my experience, they are often poor managers of people and like to leave the difficult people issues to the HR department. Every organization has some of these leaders. We need to work with them as best as possible. We need to help them see the connection between effective human resources work and the success of their domain objectives.

6. *Many line managers are averse to examining process.* I frequently come in contact with managers who are averse to examining process. They talk about not wanting to discuss process. They speak as though they will get on with their work without dealing with process. This logic always leaves me incredulous. There is nothing that they do that isn't done through process. One actually doesn't have the choice to do away with process or to carry on with life in the absence of process. But it is helpful to ask questions like, "How do we feel about the process that we have?" and "If I don't like the process that I have, am I willing to change it?"

Every business result—good or bad—is the direct result of the processes that are in place. If I don't like my current results, I had better take a very good look at my processes, because, whatever they are, they are perfectly designed to deliver these very results. Management is all about designing processes that work.

If that is true, why are so many managers averse to process? I believe there are at least two reasons. First, some just aren't wired to think in terms of process. They simply *do,* not really aware of the process they use or should use to accomplish the task. They are all about *what* and care little for *how.* The second reason that some managers have grown suspicious of process is one that I described at the end of Chapter 11. Some managers have had bad experiences with OD process fanatics and are in recovery!

So why is this reluctance to deal with process important in a conversation about human resources? Well, a great deal of human resources work—and particularly the more strategic components of human resources work—is all about process. People interact through process. Decisions are made through a process. HR people intuitively think in terms of process, because that is how human beings work: in process. HR people must stay focused on process, always looking for the process causes behind results that are off target.

An HR professional who is strategic will educate managers wanting different results on the role of process in getting those different results. But, to be effective, this must be done at a level and in language that the manager can use and digest.

7. *Diversity is not a work process but rather a subset of all aspects of human resources.* As I mentioned in Chapter 4, we had endless debates at Hallmark about how to think about diversity in the overall HR model. We decided that we would look at diversity as part of everything we did in human resources, rather than as a distinct process itself. Some felt that by not viewing diversity as a

distinct work process, we would not see it as being as important as the other human resources work processes. It is important to remember that the human resources model is not an organization chart, and therefore it says nothing about HR groups. Rather, it portrays the various processes that leverage talent to build capabilities to win in the marketplace.

When you discuss the role of diversity in human resources work, you cannot let it become a political football having to do with how highly diversity work is valued. Once the model is understood, the importance of diversity work becomes clear—it needs to be an integral part of everything done in human resources.

I am a strong believer that diversity work has to be far more than the typical diversity awareness program that has become the core of many companies' diversity effort. I believe that people make progress on areas that are important to leaders and are measured. Fortunately, our president became a strong advocate of holding leaders accountable for making a measurable difference in the number of women and people of color in executive and management positions.

I was glad that I had been tenacious on that point because our improvement was evident in our statistics. We measured representation for three different levels of leadership from officers to mid-management for women and people of color. The results were impressive. Each of these six categories showed real improvement. The smallest increase was 15 percent, and the largest was 280 percent.

Diversity work is critical. Improvement in this area has far more to do with belief and accountability than with the design of a human resources framework.

8. *HR skill gaps cannot be ignored.* Clearly, there are few things more difficult to be told than that one does not have the skills needed to do the job. Anyone who is serious about transforming

an HR group into a strategic force must be serious about the development of new skills. This issue cannot be skirted. Creating models and even redesigning the HR department will never be enough if you don't have people with the needed raw skills to get the job done.

But one of the worst things that you can do is fight for HR to have a place at the business table, succeed, and then have HR managers not know what to do once they get there. On occasion, I would ask line managers about the impact of the HR person assigned to his organization. I was always pained to hear that they didn't feel that the HR person knew how to contribute. This can set your change effort back years. You must develop strategic business and human resources skills if you are ever to transition to a truly strategic focus. Chapter 16 examined this topic much more extensively.

9. *The integration of generalist, specialist, and service center roles is very difficult.* Tension between these roles does not go away on its own and seems to be present in most organizations. Resolving this tension has much more to do with role clarification, skill development, and staffing choices than team building efforts. Chapter 14 discussed this topic in depth.

10. *Communication within HR is often weak.* We found that HR suffered from many of the same cultural and communication maladies that existed in the rest of Hallmark. I discussed some of these aspects of the culture in Chapter 11. We were not comfortable confronting hard issues. Employees at all levels were not comfortable raising questions in public forums. My staff was not comfortable disagreeing with me or with each other on issues that I felt needed our best thinking and debate.

These were basic communications habits that needed attention. I started by creating a forum for the entire HR organization that met on a quarterly basis. As I mentioned in Chapter 16, I had a line executive come each quarter to talk about the business with the HR staff. Then a key human resources topic was presented, always with time for questions and dialogue. I had to coach key people to please ask questions. Not only questions, but *hard questions*.

I also needed to model the behavior that I wanted. I needed to show the larger group that their new leader loved nothing better than having people ask hard, insightful questions that caused us to get better at some aspect of our work. I tried to model the same behavior by using a "managing by walking around" style. I especially tried to focus on key early to midcareer professionals who were considered high-potential. I would stop by their offices to talk, to ask for their help on something I was considering. I enjoyed just sitting with them and talking about a variety of topics. I wanted them to learn that you don't need to have all the answers when dealing with the head of HR. We wanted to create an environment where people wanted to work together on issues.

Know What You Stand For and What You Believe

Facing all of the challenges I've described is much easier when you are firmly grounded in what you believe. Throughout your career, you will have choices to make between the expedient and your deeply held beliefs. Classic examples have to do with business and personal ethics. Unfortunately, we live in a time when many key business leaders have allowed their uncontrolled passion for wealth and power to become so overwhelming that they have put entire corporations at risk. But issues that compromise personal integrity are usually less dramatic, things like concealing information, giving people the reports they want rather than telling them what is true, or allowing professional relationships to go beyond deeply held beliefs of what is appropriate. I believe that challenges to our personal beliefs come very subtly, generally with a certain logic that at the moment seems to make sense.

This is the case with anything that we come to rationalize. Unfortunately, we live in a society that is becoming more and more comfortable with changing the definition of integrity instead of changing the behavior when there is incongruence between the two.

For the purposes of this book, I am not interested in prescribing any particular view on where these lines should be drawn. I believe most people, with belief systems from many different origins, have a structure of beliefs about appropriate behavior and professional practices that would build, rather than destroy, organizations. My far greater concern is that whatever the particular belief structures, too many people seem to lay them aside far too quickly for the expedient or enticing. Business is in great need of leaders who are clear about their personal beliefs and ethics and who have the courage to stand by them, regardless of the costs.

In addition to personal beliefs and ethics, it is equally important and often equally challenging to have clarity about the stands that one intends to take from a strictly professional point of view. In many ways, this question is at the heart of leadership, particularly in a field in the process of significant change. This is a field that needs leaders who are willing to push the edge to create change, regardless of the perceived or real risks. The field needs leaders who are skilled at pushing the boundaries without pushing so hard that they lose their influence in the system. At the same time, we need leaders who are able to recognize when they have become an integral part of the very system that they are trying to change. We need leaders who know the point at which they are willing to walk away from an effort or even a job if critical professional standards are compromised. This could not be more challenging.

I know this from personal experience. I have left remarkably good jobs over professional differences. I left one job because of an HR leader who was such a significant obstacle to the department's ability to perform in a strategic way that I felt that deep professional boundaries had been crossed. I left another great job because of line managers who were unwilling to have HR play a direct role in the development of business strategy.

So how does one manage some of these political dynamics? It cannot be done with an overly dogmatic, black-and-white view of the world that has no flexibility at all. I believe that the following principles may help:

- Know with clarity those issues that you consider to be ethical questions, both personally and professionally.

- Know beforehand how you will react if (when) these issues arise. Anyone who believes that she won't face ethical dilemmas in her career is naïve. Anyone who faces them without having predetermined what her response will be is in a precarious position.

- Identify those professional principles and standards that are absolutes for you, those that you would quit before violating.

- Have the courage to follow your personal and professional standards.

- Know the standards that you are willing to be flexible about as part of the process of change and improvement. Anyone who expects the organization to fit his exact expectations immediately is naïve. It won't. You will need to change with the organization over time.

- Be patient. Understand that people and organizations change slowly. Real HR leaders are patient in laying out a plan for change that is not immediate, as long as their personal or professional absolutes are not being violated. At the same time, they have a healthy sense of impatience to push for movement and change.

- Know the culture of the organization in which you work. The culture will offer clues to the types of personal and ethical dilemmas you may eventually confront.

CHAPTER EIGHTEEN

Managing Your Career in the Field of Strategic Human Resources

"I never did a whole day's work in my life—it was all fun."

—THOMAS A. EDISON

"It is amazing what can be accomplished when nobody cares about who gets the credit."

—ROBERT YATES

"If a man does only what is required of him, he is a slave. If a man does more than is required of him, he is a free man."

—CHINESE PROVERB

THERE ARE MYRIAD WAYS that people think about their work. Managing your own career is fundamentally about personal preferences, interests, and priorities. I have counseled many people in human resources on career management, and the conversations are very individual. These discussions are difficult to capture in a book. But I have given a lot of thought to careers in human resources, spent time with a wide variety of successful HR leaders, and learned from

245

their career evolutions. From these experiences, I have identified the following principles for managing a successful career in the field of strategic human resources:

- Service is an honorable endeavor.

- Get as much education as early as possible.

- Learn about business.

- Don't look for a career map. This field is still in the process of being created. You will likely play a key role in its evolution.

- Focus on getting experience early in your career.

- Be prepared to pump gas.

Though individual circumstances and strengths vary, these principles generally hold true for most careers in strategic human resources. I share them, wishing that I were sitting alone with the reader in something of a career counseling session.

> *Service is an honorable endeavor.* In graduate school, I had a class with Gene Dalton, one of the founding fathers in the study of careers. He did a wonderful job of helping a group of us students assess our real interests as we left graduate school in the hope of aligning us with our best career match. When he came to me, he told me that he was perplexed and that he wasn't sure if I would be best suited to the field of human resources and organization development or if I should pursue a general management course. He said that I seemed off the chart for an HR person in terms of interest in results and management. The piece of my profile that ultimately led him to support my desires to move into organization development and human resources was my high interest in being of service to other people.

> I have come over the years to understand the importance of this for successful HR people. You must enjoy serving. You have to

have a personality that is quite comfortable doing lots of your work behind the scenes to help others be successful. You have to be able to enjoy giving others the credit. You have to be comfortable helping managers both appear good and become good at what they do.

While I suspect and hope that we will see more CEOs come from the ranks of HR, it is certainly a rare occurrence today. I suspect that the day will come when insight into organization and the management of people will become a decisive criterion for the top job. There is, however, a dilemma for HR leaders. While in the HR role, you need to feel very comfortable being in the support role. You have to enjoy helping others become successful and be able to see your success within theirs. If you have a strong desire to be on center stage, to be in control, to call the shots, or to be in the limelight, you may want to consider another field. There is a considerable need for line leaders who have a strong understanding of human resources and organization development.

Enjoying a service role does not mean that you don't want to accomplish a lot. Not at all. I have a very high need to accomplish and to make a difference. My interest is high to help others to set and accomplish an expansive vision and aggressive goals. I just don't need to always be visible or to be the focal point. I have found that that combination works remarkably well. I ultimately consider myself to be in a service business. I love to focus on my customer and help her succeed.

Get as much education as early as possible. Most business leaders do not want an overly academic HR function. They want an HR group that is practical. While I agree that HR should not come across as overly theoretical and academic, at the same time, strategic HR professionals should get as much education as possible as early as possible. The trick is in learning to translate good, robust theory into practical language and methodologies so that it can be used. Clearly, education is of little help if it becomes an obstacle to your ability to connect with management.

Education for an HR professional can include any or all of the human resources arenas. The more domain knowledge one has, the better. In particular, you would be well served to study organization theory and change methodology at some point in your development. I say this because many organizations already have a reasonably good understanding of the other domain arenas of human resources. There are still too many HR groups that do not have a good understanding of organizational dynamics and the change processes. These areas of learning also build the ability to develop overall strategic and systemic skills, skills that can be used in every aspect of human resources and in business in general.

Learn about business. This may be one of the most important developmental objectives for serious HR professionals. As I have emphasized throughout this book, you have to understand the general flow of business if you intend to play a strategic role in a business setting. Too many of those who don't learn the basics of business tend to evolve into a role of protecting employees from the business as opposed to integrating the talents of people into business success.

Ideally, I would recommend that students just thinking about entering the human resources field make sure that there is a rigorous business segment in their studies. This could come through an undergraduate degree in business or economics, with graduate work focused more specifically on human resources and organizational studies. Some academic programs include human resources/organization development as a specialty path of an MBA program. That can be fine, but make sure that this doesn't leave you without depth in either business or human resources.

More important is what you do once inside an organization. You have to take time to immerse yourself in the business. Some HR people are intimidated by business issues because they don't understand the rigorous analytics and math. That is not a good reason to shy away from business. If it is hard to understand, take time to ask for help. If you don't make the effort to understand the business, you simply will never play a truly strategic HR role. You cannot fake it, either. It will be clear by your contribution at the table whether or not you really grasp the business.

My experience is that most line leaders are more than happy to talk about their arena of work. Whenever I enter a new organization, I always ask a key financial person to walk me through the basics of finance for that organization, including these areas:

- The budgeting process

- Capital management

- Reports

- The accounting system

- Development and management of the P&L and income statements

- The measurement systems of the organization

Get in touch with the product. Spend time with the engineers or those in product development. Understand the following areas:

- The development process

- Skills needed to do the work of product development

- Where the technology is moving

- How the company moves from innovation and concept to product testing and rollout

- What it's like to work on the manufacturing line

- The distribution processes of the company

Get in touch with the marketing and sales processes of the company, and understand these points:

- How do we think about the marketplace?

- How is it segmented?

- How do we communicate with the marketplace to understand shifting expectations?

- How do we develop advertising?

- What is the sales process? Take time to ride with salespeople so that you can see firsthand how the sale is made.

- What is the product/service process of the company?

Learn the corporate processes and how these functions are handled:

- Strategic planning

- Measurement

- Communications

- Cross-division interdependencies

- Corporate governance

- Board operations

Spend time with employees, and understand their views:

- What do they feel best about?

- What are their greatest concerns?

- What do they look for in a company?

- Are they invited/allowed to contribute all the skills that they have?

There are other questions specific to your organization or industry that you should develop and find the answers to.

As you take time learning your organization, do it in a way that teaches you to understand the human and organizational implications of what you see. As you explore the processes of product, marketing, sales, manufacturing, distribution, and strategy development of the organization, continually ask yourself what the impact of this business process is upon human resources systems and processes. Ask yourself how human resources systems and practices might impact each of these business systems. This is the thought process that should be working in your head every day that you come to work. How can HR impact the business, and how does the business impact human resources work?

I suggest that you immerse yourself in business literature and not just work explicitly written about human resources. As you read the *Wall Street Journal, Business Week, Forbes*, or academic business journals, read with an eye toward the human resources implications of the issue being discussed. This is the skill that strategic HR professionals must learn. It must become second nature to them. When I interview a person, it is immediately obvious if they are practiced in this process of interpreting all business issues into human resources implications. The good ones do it without even thinking. Others don't make the connection at all.

Don't look for a career map. This field is still in the process of being created. You will likely play a key role in its evolution. As I mentioned in Chapter 2, when I made the transition from OD to HR, I was scared to death. I was scared to move from something that I knew I could succeed at to something that felt full of risk. The first lifeline that I looked for was a book about how to succeed at strategic human resources. When I couldn't find the book, I started looking for people who could become my mentor, someone who had done it. I found precious few in the mid-1980s and early 1990s. One of my most freeing days was the day that I realized that the expert didn't exist, that I would have to create many of the models and constructs that I would use.

I believe that if you are looking for the detailed roadmap, you will be disappointed and waste a lot of time in the process. Learn principles, and then go out and apply them with reason and with an eye toward learning from what works and what doesn't work.

This is one of the many reasons that I think this is a great field to enter. There is still a lot of room to create and move the field. It is a field in real need of leaders who are able to be creative, innovative, and bold in their leadership.

The job that I left at Hallmark didn't even exist when I left graduate school. The job that most future HR leaders will retire from doesn't exist today. Most fun of all is that you will be part of designing it.

Focus on getting experience early in your career; do it because you love it. Too many young people enter their career fields far too focused upon money and job level. This misses the point. My recommendation to people early in their careers is to focus on experience. You should get as much good experience as fast as you can. Don't worry about money. Don't worry about titles or offices. Give your time away if you need to. Volunteer to work on projects. Do extra effort at any opportunity. I am a believer in career leverage. By that I mean that you should do anything you can to "work over your head." Get that little bit of experience that others aren't getting. Do something that will differentiate you from the rest. When the first promotion opportunities come up, all of this extra experience that you have packed in will enable you to get the next job, once again putting you in just a bit over your head.

Focusing on the work and experience is the best career management practice I know. Then, if money and visible recognition are important to you, they will come. I believe, however, that you will find that what drives you is the love of the work and not the money. Frankly, anyone who spends most of his time worrying more about money and title than the work should probably look for another field. As with any field, you will excel in human resources work only if you do it for the sheer enjoyment of the work. If that is not the driver, I suspect that HR could be a horrible place to spend time.

Be prepared to pump gas. We each view our careers and how to manage them differently. Since the beginning of my career, I have always given the same response to a boss who asked what my career goals were. For me, the response has always been, "I want to be able to pump gas tomorrow and feel good about myself." Generally, upon hearing this response, bosses would pause and look at me sort of funny and ask me what my career goals *really* were. I would repeat, "I want to be able to pump gas tomorrow and feel good about myself." (I don't know the origin of this concept. It has been in my head for as long as I can recall. I understand that the metaphor may be meaningless to those early in their career today, since this occupation is virtually extinct.)

Now, my preference would be to do more than pumping gas. I explained to my bosses that I refused to ever have my sense of self so wrapped up in my career—in positions, places on an organization chart, or financial achievement—that I couldn't feel good about myself without them. I never wanted to be defined as a human being by my job. I tried to explain that this framework alone would give me the mental space to do what needed to be done and say what needed to be said. The minute I let myself become dependent upon a boss for my sense of self, I was owned and would likely never take the risks that someone in the change field must be willing to take. I tried to explain that I was of far more value to the organization with a free mind-set than I could ever be otherwise.

Has this helped? Yes, it has. I have always felt free and open to say what those around me see but won't say. Does this approach come with risk? Absolutely. It is full of risk. But that is the whole purpose of this mind-set—to free you up mentally and psychologically so that you can take risks.

Think carefully about the role that your career plays in your life. What would you trade off to build your career? Are you willing to leave or be fired over a principle that you believe in? Which principles? This field is in need of leaders with vision who have a point of view and are willing to take strong stands to move that view forward. We need leaders who are wise enough to balance the risk in a way that allows them to stay alive in a system that needs their influence for change. At the same time, these leaders need to recognize the lines they will not cross, regardless of the cost.

The fact of the matter is that for the good leaders, there will always be other options. There is a paradox. I am quite convinced that those who are the best leaders are in their roles because they reflect the work that they want to do. It is not about the title or the money or the power of politics. They just love the work. I have always loved the work in this field of organization development and human resources. The fact that I also get paid to do it has been a wonderful added bonus.

CHAPTER NINETEEN

The Future of Human Resources

WHERE IS THE FIELD of human resources headed? No one knows for sure. In this chapter, I mix my beliefs and hopes with a reasonable dose of today's reality and take a stab at responding to this question.

Management will continue to emphasize the need to pay attention to the organization and human issues. I am confident that line leaders of organizations will increasingly see the need to pay attention to human and organizational issues. They are desperately trying to find ways to differentiate themselves in the marketplace. Issues of culture and work process will become more important as such differentiators. Managers will look for help in these areas wherever they can find it. If internal HR organizations have built the capability to address these key strategic business needs in ways that are measurable, CEOs will be more than happy to use these resources. I believe that they will prefer to have this type of capability inside the organization. However, if they do not have this type of strategic HR leadership and talent base inside, they will easily relegate the internal HR function to the more administrative details that they have traditionally done and will find the strategic talent outside.

255

There will continue to be a growing number of strategic HR resources to be found externally. These will be a mixed bag, as they are now. However, there will be an increasing number of people who will offer tremendous expertise and needed strategic perspectives.

HR leaders will become increasingly strategic and increasingly effective business leaders. I believe that there is nothing but opportunity for proven strategic HR leaders. The demand will continue to outstrip the supply for the foreseeable future. There is a large cadre of midlevel HR professionals in organizations today that will be ready for the top jobs of the coming decade. Many of them are ready to take their bosses' jobs today. They will be very mobile because of the demand. As a result, line and HR leaders who do not provide an environment where creative HR professionals are able to join in the strategic issues of the organization will lose their key HR talent.

Talented strategic HR leaders will find themselves increasingly in the middle of the most strategic issues in the organizations in which they work. Because of the raw value that they bring, they will be invited to participate in core business issues. More HR leaders will be invited to play other key roles in the organization, including COO and CEO. Why is this? Because boards of directors are increasingly going to look for leaders who know how to manage people, organization, and change well. Again, these will be HR leaders who have come to know the business in intimate detail.

The administrative components will become separated from HR. The administrative components of human resources are already being outsourced or moved to centralized service centers. This trend will continue. More and more we will see these centers providing all administrative work for the entity, not just HR. Current functional service centers will be combined. These megaservice centers will handle administration for finance, HR, purchasing, and other functions. The strategic components of human resources will remain at the heart of the HR function.

New attention will be paid to employee relations and workforce planning. While a more strategic view has been taken in certain areas of human resources such as organization development, learning and development, and performance management, bright new HR leaders will apply this same creative and strategic thinking to the other aspects of human resources. Two areas that I believe are both critical and just waiting for leadership are workforce planning and employee relations. Workforce planning may seem tedious to some, but doing it well will be viewed as having critical leverage going forward. Having the right workforce will be one of the most important aspects of HR in the future. Companies will be built and will die over this issue. The HR leaders who can step in and design these processes will be highly valued.

Employee relations is also a crucial aspect of human resources. This has always been so, but we are about to see a significant revamping of how this work and function are viewed. I believe that HR will focus less on union management, policy, and paternalistic relationships with employees. Instead, HR will introduce exciting new ways to think about the relationship between the employee and the entity. This relationship will be built upon principles of trust and integrity. Both management and employees will come to understand that being trusted requires behaving in a trustworthy manner.

This will create an employee/management relationship that will be based upon a mature exchange of needed skills for needed work. It will minimize the paternalistic relationship that often exists today. It will assume that employees are adults who can manage their careers, rather than children who need to have decisions made for them. It will focus on the ongoing development of new skills and abilities for workers. It will create an environment where employees are mobile. Loyalty will be expressed by employees who are doing everything in their power to make the entity more effective, not by employees who simply plan to always be there.

The field will learn how to measure its performance. While there are those in academia who have worked hard to understand how to measure human resources work and results, we still have a long way to go. I confess that I have done little to advance this area of human resources in my career. The one thing that I did, however, was to always keep human resources work connected to the business results in the hearts of line leaders.

In my last several years at Hallmark, I began using my personal performance review as a surrogate for the HR function's performance. In essence, my objectives and commitment to the president to deliver certain work represented his expectations of the HR division. Of course, there were a few aspects of my personal review that remained individual. But I assumed that 90 percent of my review was the department's review. I let the president know that that was how I intended to think about my review. I encouraged him to give messages to the HR department as he gave messages to me. I then presented my performance review to the entire HR organization as representing the president's assessment of them and me.

It was actually a remarkable experience. I was able to let the various subgroups of HR know exactly how company leadership felt about our work. Either we were delivering value or we were not. Either the HR organization and I were aligned or we were not. I suspect that people far smarter than I am will come up with much better measures than this in the future, but there was something rather straightforward in this approach.

I hope that the primary advances in measurement will be in the ability to directly link human resources efforts to the success of the company in the marketplace. I believe we will come up with measures that answer the question "Does this HR effort make any difference to our end-user customer?"

There will be a renewed emphasis on human life principles. I believe that we will begin to deal with aspects of the human experience that are all too often simply not part of the business vocabulary and experience, yet are at the core of humanity. These are human qualities that have been taught in most cultures, philosophies, and religions that have helped societies not only to survive but to prosper. I believe that there are several human attributes that are critical for societies of any type to prosper. They include these:

- *Respect.* Respect for each other as human beings is crucial and all too often missing in the fast-paced organizational life in which we live. This does not mean that we need to become alike in order to show respect. In fact, respect is most powerfully shown when there are differences. Unfortunately, there are too many who suggest that we can respect each other only when we all become alike, when we taste more like a puree than a rich vegetable stew. We need to validate our differences in a way that lets us be legitimately different rather than demanding that we all become some average of the whole.

- *Honesty.* This may seem simplistic, but we need to learn to tell the truth. I am amazed at how many good people in good organizations have learned to describe the world as they or their leaders want it to be, rather than honestly describing what is real. Until we can be comfortable telling the truth, we will never create effective organizations.

- *Humility.* History is replete with the downfall of entire civilizations that have become proud and certain that they can stand independent and rely solely upon their own capabilities. This has never worked in the long run in the past and will not in the future. We need leaders and individual contributors who have the humility to know and admit what they don't know, to know and admit when they make a mistake, to know and admit when they can learn from someone else.

- *Forgiveness.* We need to understand that all of us make mistakes. Until we can institutionalize the ability to forgive and let people move on, we will always short-circuit the power of people and organizations.

- *Excellence.* We need to create cultures that strive in everything they do to become excellent, to become better. We need to overcome the temptation to put up with mediocrity.

- *Service.* We need to understand that service to others is a virtue, not a burden. Leaders need to learn the paradox that they are the ultimate servants.

I will let you add to this list. I simply believe that we need to bring back into the business language and mind-set a whole arena of human development that is generally left untouched in business.

We seem to think that these questions of ethics and morals have no place in business. But they are the fabric of the human condition. They are real. It is a drastic mistake to suggest that these principles have no place in business. They are at the foundation of business, and yet we rarely teach and emphasize them. I hope HR will help to make these principles real in a way that is not simply cheerleading but is clearly connected to the quality of the business and people's experience inside the organization.

This will be a great field to work in. Finally, I deeply believe that HR will be a great place to work in the coming decade. The evolution that has been described in part in this book is far from complete. I truly hope that no one reads this book as a complete description of how to do strategic human resources. It is not. There is an incredible amount of room for new and creative thinking in the field. There is a deep need for bold and strong leaders who are willing to step outside traditional ways of working and see and create the future of human resources.

Recommended Readings

Strategy

- Christensen, Clayton M. *The Innovator's Dilemma.* New York: HarperBusiness, 2003.

- ———, and Michael E. Raynor. *The Innovator's Solution: Creating and Sustaining Successful Growth.* Boston: Harvard Business School Press, 2003.

- Collins, Jim. *Good to Great: Why Some Companies Make the Leap . . . and Others Don't.* New York: HarperBusiness, 2001.

- ———, and Jerry I. Porras. *Built to Last: Successful Habits of Visionary Companies.* New York: HarperBusiness, 2002.

- Collis, David J., Cynthia A. Montgomery, Michael Goold, Andrew Campbell, C. K. Prahalad, Kenneth Lieberthal, and Stuart L. Hart. *Harvard Business Review on Corporate Strategy.* Boston: Harvard Business School Press, 1999.

- Goold, Michael, Andrew Campbell, and Marcus Alexander. *Corporate-Level Strategy: Creating Value in the Multibusiness Company.* New York: Wiley, 1994.

- Hamel, Gary, and C. K. Prahalad. *Competing for the Future.* Boston: Harvard Business School Press, 1996.

- Henderson, Bruce D. *Henderson on Corporate Strategy.* New York: Harper & Row, 1979.

- Kaplan, Robert, Kathy Eisenhardt, Don Sull, Peter Tufano, Orit Gadiesh, James Gilbert, Mohanbir Sawhney, and Michael Porter. *Harvard Business Review on Advances in Strategy.* Boston: Harvard Business School Press, 2002.

- Mintzberg, Henry, Joseph B. Lampel, James Brian Quinn, and Sumantra Ghoshal. *The Strategy Process.* Upper Saddle River, N.J.: Prentice Hall, 2002.

- Porter, Michael E. *Competitive Advantage of Nations.* New York: Free Press, 1998.

- ———. *Competitive Strategy: Techniques for Analyzing Industries and Competitors.* New York: Free Press, 1998.

- ———. *Michael E. Porter on Competition* Boston: Harvard Business School Press, 1998.

- ———. "What is Strategy?" *Harvard Business Review*, February 2000.

- Slywotzky, Adrian J., David J. Morrison, and Bob Andelman. *The Profit Zone: How Strategic Business Design Will Lead You to Tomorrow's Profits.* New York: Three Rivers Press, 2002.

- Slywotzky, Adrian J. *Value Migration: How to Think Several Moves Ahead of the Competition* Boston: Harvard Business School Press, 1996.

- Wiersema, Fred. *The New Market Leaders: Who's Winning and How in the Battle for Customers.* New York: Free Press, 2001.

Human Resources

- Becker, Brian E., Mark A. Huselid, and Dave Ulrich. *The HR Scorecard: Linking People, Strategy, and Performance.* Boston: Harvard Business School Press, 2001.

- Charan, Ram, Stephen Drotter, and James Noel. *The Leadership Pipeline: How to Build the Leadership-Powered Company.* San Francisco: Jossey-Bass, 2001.

- Fitz-enz, Jac. *How to Measure Human Resource Management.* New York: McGraw-Hill, 2001.

- ———. *Human Value Management: The Value-Adding Human Resource Management Strategy for the 1990s.* San Francisco: Pfeiffer, 1990.

- ———. *The ROI of Human Capital: Measuring the Economic Value of Employee Performance.* New York: AMACOM Books, 2000.

- Kravetz, Dennis J. *The Human Resources Revolution: Implementing Progressive Management Practices for Bottom Line Success.* New York: Jossey-Bass, 1988.

- Ulrich, Dave, ed. *Delivering Results: A New Mandate for HR Professionals.* Boston: Harvard Business School Press, 1998.

- ———. *Human Resource Champions.* Boston: Harvard Business School Press, 1997.

- ———, Michael R. Losey, and Gerry Lake, eds. *Tomorrow's HR Management: 48 Thought Leaders Call for Change.* New York: Wiley, 1997.

- ———, and Norm Smallwood, *Why the Bottom Line ISN'T!: How to Build Value Through People and Organization.* New York: Wiley, 2003.

Organizational Behavior

- Black, J. Stewart, and Hal B. Gregersen. *Leading Strategic Change: Breaking Through the Brain Barrier.* London: Financial Times/Prentice Hall Books, 2003.

- Block, Peter. *Flawless Consulting: A Guide to Getting Your Expertise Used.* New York: Pfeiffer, 1999.

- Drucker, Peter. *Managing in a Time of Great Change.* New York: Plume Books, 1998.

- French, Wendell L., and Cecil H. Bell. *Organization Development: Behavioral Science Interventions for Organization Improvement.* Upper Saddle River, N.J.: Prentice Hall, 1998.

- Kotter, John P. *Force for Change: How Leadership Differs from Management.* New York: Free Press, 1990.

- ———. *Leading Change.* Boston: Harvard Business School Press, 1996.

- Moss Kanter, Rosabeth. *Change Masters.* New York: Free Press, 1985.

- Patterson, Kerry, Joseph Grenny, Al Switzler, and Ron McMillan. *The Balancing Act: Mastering the Competing Demands of Leadership.* New York: Thompson Executive Press, 1996.

- Quinn, James Brian. *Strategies for Change: Logical Incrementalism.* Homewood, Ill.: R. D. Irwin, 1980.

- Senge, Peter M., Charlotte Roberts, George Roth, Bryan Smith, and Richard B. Ross. *The Dance of Change: The Challenges of Sustaining Momentum in a Learning Organization.* New York: Random House, 1999.

- ———. *The Fifth Discipline: The Art and Practice of The Learning Organization.* New York: Doubleday, 1994.

Index